The Relationship Worlds of Infants and Toddlers

The Relationship Worlds of Infants and Toddlers

Multiple Perspectives from Early Years Theory and Practice

Sheila Degotardi and Emma Pearson

 Open University Press

Open University Press
McGraw-Hill Education
McGraw-Hill House
Shoppenhangers Road
Maidenhead
Berkshire
England
SL6 2QL

email: enquiries@openup.co.uk
world wide web: www.openup.co.uk

and Two Penn Plaza, New York, NY 10121-2289, USA

First published 2014
Copyright © Sheila Degotardi and Emma Pearson, 2014

A catalogue record of this book is available from the British Library

ISBN-13: 978-0-33-526300-4 (pb)
ISBN-10: 0-33-526300-3 (pb)
eISBN: 978-0-33-526301-1

Library of Congress Cataloging-in-Publication Data
CIP data applied for

Typesetting and e-book compilations by
RefineCatch Limited, Bungay, Suffolk
Printed and bound by CPI Group (UK) Ltd, Croydon, CR0 4YY

Praise for this book

"This book invites the reader into the life lived by infants and toddlers as they engage and negotiate with their significant others and with each other, in out of home formal early childhood settings. It can be seen throughout each chapter that infants are social from a very early age, and it would appear, very keen to be in the company of others, communicating exactly what they want and need and contributing to a relationship. The authors advise that, the quality of the response of the adult to the infant's or toddler's bids for connection with others, should be respectful, sensitive and 'intune' with the child's emotional state, forming secure, long term relationships which ultimately contribute to the child's and the child's family's, sense of trust, security and well-being within the setting. This book of quite unique Australian research, alerts the teachers of young children, early childhood students and families, that infancy and toddler-hood are unique phases of life and not to be dismissed or overlooked as the writers show that children seek and engage in profound relationships with adults other than family members."

Wendy Shepherd, Institute of Early Childhood,
Macquarie University, Australia

"We learn how to cope and adapt primarily through relationships in our first years. Degotardi and Pearson write compellingly as they endorse infant-toddler participatory rights and concepts such as togetherness and cooperation. They achieve a balance in collating theoretical, research and practice-based knowledge while providing thoughtful analyses. This book will be enlightening for under- and post-graduate students, it is essential for teachers' pedagogy, and a valued text for anyone in the education world. Communication is at the heart of being human and the authors' approaches to understanding relationships will assists us in that endeavour."

Jean Rockel, Editor, The First Years Nga Tau Tuatahi
Journal of Infant and Toddler Education

"There is increasing global interest in research studies of infants and toddlers in day care. Drawing on their own research studies Degotardi and Pearson ask deeply critical questions about how we can make sense of the relationship worlds of the youngest citizens in our society. With over thirty years' experience of working in practice, policy and research roles with infant and toddlers, the words 'Relationships are complicated' imme-diately resonated with me. This book is a must read for all those who, like me, have an enduring fascination in the lives of infants and toddlers."

Dr Jools Page, University of Sheffield, UK

To our partners, families, friends, colleagues and students, and to the educators, children and families who participated in our research, thank you.

Contents

Foreword

Liz Brooker

I was pleased and rather flattered to be asked, a few months ago, to read and comment on the chapters of this book and to write a brief introduction. Flattered, in particular, because I consider myself a latecomer to the worlds of infants and toddlers, which the authors and many of their colleagues have been exploring for so long. I have learned so much from their research and writings, and from our few opportunities to meet and talk face to face, that commenting on their work felt like dipping my toe into a rather large ocean. Nevertheless, having ventured into this world myself in recent years, I am delighted to have the chance to say something about the contribution they make in this book.

My own late coming to the study of children under the age of 3, and especially of infants and toddlers, has been by a circuitous route. Rather than starting out from child development and moving into the social and cultural worlds of the youngest children, I began my life as an educational researcher while I was a primary school teacher, working with children aged 4 and 5. As I began to examine children's transitions into school, I wondered why I had ignored the transitions that children make in their earliest months and years: into crèche, baby room, toddler room, playgroup and eventually, at the grand age of 3 years old, into preschool or nursery (which in England is the experience of about 98 per cent of children). I took the opportunities offered by a number of London nurseries and Children's Centres to study the experiences of children aged from a few months old to 3 years, mostly by observations shared with the children's parents and educators. My conclusions, like those of the present authors, were that transitions for children of this age were a process of *relationship formation*, and that if this dimension of the experience was 'got right', most children could cope well with all the other dimensions that transition-researchers identify as problematic (physical environment, care routines, curriculum, pedagogy, separation, and so on).

As I continued to focus on identifying how very young children constructed relationships with others, I was delighted to be contacted by a research team at Charles Sturt University in Australia and invited to join a week-long seminar that brought me into the world of the real international experts – including Sheila Degotardi. Despite the awesome difficulties of distance, members of the group assembled there have managed to stay in touch, and even to meet up in Europe and in England to sustain the thinking that occurred in that memorable week.

What makes this work, and this book, so special? For me it is the recognition that very young children's identity – their sense of who they are and where they belong – is established from birth through the kinds of relationship they experience with adults and peers. As Sheila Degotardi and Emma Pearson demonstrate, each relationship can be viewed as having a range of functions and dimensions (and each relationship is different from every other). But to the infant or small child, what matters is the affirmation of their selfhood, as they begin to learn that they are a separate person from their caregivers, and that they are a unique individual while at the same time sharing characteristics with other individuals and groups. Early relationships are the means by which children discover that they have a name, that they belong to a family, and that there are others who care for them and about them: in short, that they are important. (As we know from studies of orphans and refugees, children whose lives begin in such adverse circumstances that no one affirms their importance face a very difficult growing-up experience). As relationships spread to include peers and siblings, children learn more about what makes them similar to, and different from, other boys/girls, and from older or younger children, bigger or smaller children, more and less skilled children. Through these relationships an important network of interdependence grows, in which each child's needs and competencies, dependence and independence, makes a contribution to the whole.

The role of early educators is crucial, as Degotardi and Pearson show through their own examples, in supporting and sustaining this network. The observations they present from their research vividly demonstrate the many different functions and dimensions of teaching and caregiving: in responding contingently to the interests and wishes that even the youngest pre-verbal children express; in creating a triangle of care with parents and community members; and in promoting and strengthening children's relations with other children and adults, including their own family members. Thinking about these closely observed incidents brought to mind Axel Honneth's (1995) concept of *recognition*, and the three levels of recognition that secure children's sense of belonging and support their developing identity. The first level, *personal recognition*, is revealed in the strong and positive relationships offered by family members and educators, which support children in acquiring the confidence to access the other two levels of recognition: the *recognition of their rights* and the *recognition of their community*. The second level is achieved through having one's legal rights secured and safeguarded, through action and advocacy. When families live in disadvantaged circumstances, it may fall to educators to secure children's rights to all the social, educational and welfare benefits to which they are entitled – to establish children's legitimate place in the wider society. In building respectful and reciprocal relationships with parents, early educators help to consolidate children's relationship with their parents and affirm their entitlement. The third level described by Honneth is recognition by one's community, in this case the community of the setting. As children transition into group care, their new community needs to provide opportunities that enable children to feel safe and secure, to affiliate to their group and to develop a kind of solidarity with their peers.

Theorizing relationships in this way can make them sound simple, but as Degotardi and Pearson show, this is not the case: relationships are complex and infinitely various. The research they have jointly undertaken, and the observations they discuss in the following chapters, affirm that forming relationships is the most significant trigger to young children's development of a positive identity, and thus to their long-term wellbeing.

1 Relationships in early years settings: definitions and challenges

> *Relationships are complicated.*
>
> Robert Hinde

For the majority of us, relationships form one of the most important aspects of our lives. Throughout our lives, the relationships we experience have a major bearing on how, why and when we communicate, who we care for and how others care for us, how we work, play, teach and learn, and how we organize our social and professional lives. Relationships with others also provide the basis through which we learn social and cultural ways of behaving and thinking that shape our present and, through our interactions with others, are likely to influence future generations. Our immersion in relationships with others therefore defines who we are and how we are perceived, whether that be as friend, partner, parent, teacher, learner, colleague, group member and so on.

It is therefore not surprising that there is an abundance of professional and research books on human relationships that span many different disciplines, including developmental and social psychology (e.g. Hinde, 1997; Noller, Feeney and Peterson, 2001; Vangelisti and Perlman, 2006; Forgas and Fitness, 2008), clinical and health sciences (e.g. Brecht, 1997; Welsh, 2003; Meier and Rovers, 2010), organizational psychology (e.g. Baker, 2009; Shore, Coyle-Shapiro and Tetrick, 2012), cultural studies (e.g. Gudykunst, Ting-Toomey and Nishida, 1996) and others too numerous to mention in this context. A commitment to the significance of relationships also has widespread appeal and support in early childhood education, where phrases like 'relationship-based curriculum', 'teaching and learning through relationships' and 'relational pedagogy' abound in professional, policy and research literature. In many aspects of contemporary professional and personal life, 'relationships', it would seem, is a very hot topic!

Yet in three words, Robert Hinde (1997, p. 11) summed up a major challenge faced by anyone who wishes to understand the nature and significance of human relationships. *Relationships are complicated.* From the moment of birth, humans are immersed in and shaped by many relationships with different people, across various contexts, in their lives. The relationships that any individual establishes are each qualitatively different, not only in form, but also in function. This form and function will change over time, as the individuals involved grow in age and experience. And these relationships have unique meanings for each individual, as all individuals bring their previous experiences, needs, priorities and expectations to the process of relationship-building.

It is the complexity that underpins relationships that we explore in this book. We focus on the context of formalized infant–toddler education and care,[1] where the significance of relationships in young children's lives, learning and wellbeing has become a focus of increasing attention in research and practice. However, while there is widespread agreement that relationships do matter for infant–toddler development and wellbeing, there is a need to develop a more comprehensive knowledge base about *what* these relationships look and feel like, *how* they should be fostered, and *why* they are important for the children, educators and families involved in the infant–toddler programme. In this book we aim to contribute to building this knowledge base by approaching the topic of relationships in infant–toddler early childhood and care settings from a range of different perspectives. In particular, we ask the following questions.

- Which kinds of relationships are important in infant–toddler early education and care settings?
- How can we conceptualize the characteristics of these relationships?
- How can we understand the meaning of these relationships for individuals and groups?
- How can we use our understandings to build relationships in infant–toddler programmes that will benefit children, families and educators?

For those with a vested interest in supporting the development and maintenance of relationships, these are important questions. They are important because the way in which relationships are conceptualized and prioritized in any given context will have a flow-on effect to the kinds of relationships that are promoted in that setting. In other words, the relationship perspectives held by individuals and groups will determine which relationships they recognize and which they overlook or discourage, as well as the efforts that are put in place to foster the relationships that are deemed significant to current and future functioning.

What is 'a relationship'?

A good place to start this exploration of relationship complexity is with a definition. At its most basic, a relationship can be characterized as a form of attraction or mutual liking – a sense of magnetism that either brings people together or keeps them apart. While this conceptualization of a relationship is popular in romantic fiction, its one-dimensional simplicity masks the complex processes that are involved in forming and maintaining interpersonal relationships. By focusing on basic attraction, we remove the relationship from the individual, social and cultural forces that make up people's real-world existences. We ignore individual factors such as priorities, interests and understandings, and negate the importance of the interactions, behaviours, activities and routines that take place within a social-cultural system of beliefs and practices. By focusing on simple attraction, we run the risk of characterizing a relationship as something that happens effortlessly, without having to be built and maintained, without any personal or shared judgements and without the influence of understandings that are constructed over time (Duck, 1999). This is not the reality of the relationships world.

A more comprehensive way of defining a relationship can be found in Hinde's (1979) foundational and influential work, which endeavoured to understand the nature and constituent parts of interpersonal relationships. Hinde firmly situates relationships in people's social world by attributing a central role to *interpersonal interactions*. For these interactions to have relationship potential, Hinde argues that they must move beyond one-off, functional interactions to involve a sense of *mutuality* as each partner responds to the behaviours and communications of the other. A significant feature of such interactions is that they occur over extended periods of *time*, and therefore provide some degree of continuity. Importantly, each successive interaction is affected by what has occurred in the past, and may affect the interactions that will take place in the future. A relationship is therefore not only built through interactions, but also is founded on each individual's *knowledge* of the other and their *expectations* of kinds of interactions that they are likely to have. In this way, Hinde explains how relationships can stand the test of time because, even after absences, 'the accumulated effects of past interactions will ensure that when they next meet, they do not see each other as strangers' (Hinde, 1979, p. 15).

Hinde (1979) thus draws attention to internal, psychological aspects of relationships, as the relationship quality is not only dependent on the occurrence of interactions, but also on what each person *thinks about* what occurred during those interactions. In other words, the relationships that we have had in the past, and our interpretations of those relationships, will influence the nature of our relationships into the future. Every person you meet has a history of relationships that will influence your own developing relationship with that person. Relationships therefore comprise a complex system of interactions, behaviours, thoughts and understandings, all of which have personal meaning for the individuals involved. For this reason, to fully appreciate the complexity of relationships, 'it is necessary to come to terms not only with their behavioural but also with their affective/cognitive aspects, and to do so whilst recognising that they are inextricably interwoven' (Hinde, 1979, p. 15).

The significance of relationships

The central role that relationships play in human existence is highlighted by an almost universal acceptance that relationships have a pervasive and long-lasting influence on people's social, emotional and psychological wellbeing (Lamb, 2005; Lewis, 2005). This recognition is particularly strong in early childhood, as a large body of multi-disciplinary evidence demonstrates that infants and toddlers flourish when they experience warm, caring and stimulating relationships with significant others in their lives. A decade ago, the National Scientific Council on the Developing Child introduced a working paper that drew together the implications of this extensive body of research for young children's learning and development, as follows:

> Young children experience their world as an environment of relationships, and these relationships affect virtually all aspects of their development – intellectual, social, emotional, physical, behavioral, and moral. The quality and stability of a child's human relationships in the early years lay the foundation for a wide range of later developmental outcomes that really matter – self-confidence and sound mental health, motivation to learn, achievement in school and later in life, the ability to control aggressive impulses and resolve conflicts in non-violent ways, knowing the difference between right and wrong, having the capacity to develop and sustain casual friendships and intimate relationships, and ultimately to be a successful parent oneself.
>
> (National Scientific Council on
> the Developing Child, 2004, p. 1)

With such far-reaching implications for young children's development and wellbeing, it is not surprising that many different theoretical perspectives have been used to conceptualize and investigate the topic of young children's relationships. Psychoanalytic perspectives have contributed to our understanding of how children's first relationships can impact their social and emotional wellbeing, as well as influence their approaches to learning (e.g. Bowlby, 1969/2000; Ainsworth, 1979). Socio-cultural and socio-constructivist explanations place children's participation in the social activities of their community at the centre of their development and learning processes, and propose that, through interactions, children both reflect and creatively transform their culture (e.g. Corsaro, 1994; Rogoff, 2003). Social-cognitive theories have been used to investigate how children's developing understanding of self and others impacts on their abilities to engage in close, connected and coordinated interactions with others (e.g. Dunn, 1994; Carpendale and Lewis, 2006). And neurobiological research not only demonstrates how certain capacities for learning are 'hard-wired' into our brains, but also that a crucial ingredient in the dynamic interaction between genes and experience is the nature of children's participation in relationships with significant others (National Scientific Council on the Developing Child, 2007).

The contemporary lives of infants and toddlers

The importance attributed to relationships across a diversity of developmental theories provides the starting point from which to introduce this book on the relationship worlds of infants and toddlers, and the multiple perspectives that help us to grasp their significance. The contemporary lives of babies and toddlers in most industrialized contexts provide additional justification for our endeavour. Traditionally, formalized, out-of-home care and education settings for young children have been associated with attempts to provide children from households perceived as disadvantaged with interventions to ensure healthy growth and development. Some of the pioneers of early childhood education (e.g. Pestalozzi, Froebel and Montessori) based much of their work on a perceived need to protect children from potentially harmful surroundings. However, the nature and purpose of infant toddler programmes have since shifted considerably in response to socio-political and economic change as well as to advances in knowledge related to early childhood educaiton and care. Today, social and geographical mobility have resulted in families from diverse socio-economic and cultural backgrounds increasingly turning to formalized contexts for the care and education of their youngest children. In many countries, social, economic and labour market forces have been significant drivers in the increasing provision and use of out-of-home care and education services. In addition, many political and educational policies now explicitly recognize that the quality of early childhood services is pivotal in supporting children's wellbeing and development, and that both early childhood services and families can benefit from shared participation in these services (Organisation for Economic Co-operation and Development, 2006).

At the same time, the field of early childhood is increasingly influenced by scholars whose work has focused on deepening our understanding of the important inputs that families and communities, as well as formal education settings, provide for children's growth and development (Whiting and Whiting, 1975; Bronfenbrenner, 1979; Moll *et al.*, 1992). The sector has responded to these theoretical approaches by moving away from a singular focus on how best to care for and educate children within formal contexts, to a broader concern with understanding how best to align education and care for young children with their experiences and lives outside of formal provision. There is now widespread agreement that engagement of family and community in formalized settings forms an important aspect of quality in early childhood education and care. For these reasons, it is imperative that the nature and significance of the relationships that occur within early childhood education and care programmes are understood in relation to, and in the context of, family and community experiences.

Early childhood settings as a relationship-rich context

While many different theoretical perspectives can be drawn on to understand children's experiences in early years settings, contemporary approaches tend to place interactions at the heart of their learning processes. Learning is situated within a participatory framework in which new understandings are constructed through dynamic, reciprocal and responsive interactions between the child and other people, events and objects within the early childhood context (e.g. Berthelsen and Brownlee, 2005; Papatheodorou and Moyles, 2009; Thyssen, 2010). This essential role that interactions play in children's lives and learning is acknowledged in many early childhood curriculum documents through frequent references to the centrality of relationships. For example:

- the Australian Early Learning Framework, *Belonging, Being and Becoming* (Australian Department of Education Employment and Workplace Relations, 2009), lists *'Secure, respectful and reciprocal relationships'* and *'Partnerships'* as the first two of its five guiding principles, stressing that 'children are connected to family, community, culture and place' and that 'development and learning takes place through these relationships' (p. 7)
- the English Statutory Framework for *Early Years Foundation Stage* (Department of Education, 2012) has as a guiding principle that 'children learn to be strong and independent through positive relationships' (p. 3)
- the New Zealand curriculum document, *Te Whāriki* (Ministry of Education, 1996), has *'Relationships'* as one of its four key principles of learning and development, and states that *'Children learn through responsive and reciprocal relationships with people, places and things'* (Principle 4)

- the Scottish government's *Pre-birth to Three* (Learning and Teaching Scotland, 2010) nominates '*Relationships*', '*Responsive care*' and '*Respect*' as the three key pedagogical principles that underlie its approach to effective early year pedagogy
- Ireland's National Quality Framework for Early Childhood Education, *Síolta* (Centre for Early Childhood Development and Education, 2006), stresses significant relationships with peers, adults, family and community, stating that 'positive relationships, which are secure, responsive and respectful and which provide consistency and continuity over time, are the cornerstone of the child's wellbeing' (Principle 4).

These policy documents, designed to support high-quality early years practice, draw on rigorous evidence that positive early relationships are crucial to healthy development and growth, not only for their impact on other areas of development, but also for their role in shaping children's subsequent relationship experiences (Shonkoff and Phillips, 2000). In doing so, they put a premium on the ability of early childhood education and care services to support the development and strengthening of relationships between children, educators, families and communities. As Shonkoff and Phillips have stated: 'relationships, and the effect of relationships on relationships, are the building blocks of healthy development' (p. 27).

This emphasis on relationships as a central aspect of quality childcare and education is a relatively new one and, as this book seeks to highlight, is characterized in reality by profound complexities. Our own research indicates the existence of a wide range of perspectives on why, how, where and when relationships can and should be enacted and built in early childhood settings. These perspectives may differ not only across individual family, community and infant–toddler settings, but also across the types of relationship that are being considered (educator[2]–parent; educator–child; child–child; educator–educator; and so forth). Hence, the knowledge base on how best to support relationship-building in formal early childhood settings is still under development.

There are further challenges that can limit the ways in which relationship-based approaches can be designed and implemented in education and care settings. One such challenge is the ongoing influence of outdated notions of infant and toddler social competencies; in particular, notions of solitary, egocentric players and learners that, despite robust evidence to the contrary, maintain a presence in infant–toddler early childhood thinking and practice (Davis and Degotardi, in press). Any positioning of infants and toddlers as essentially pre-social will necessarily limit conceptualizations of relationships and relationship-based learning and teaching. A further challenge relates to the dominance of a narrow range of theoretical approaches, in particular the predominance of attachment theory (Degotardi and Pearson, 2009). While attachment theory and research continue to provide valuable guidance about the importance of early relationships and ways in which they can be supported, concerns have also been raised about the applicability to diverse group care contexts of what is essentially a Western, dyadic, family based theory (Cortazar and Herreros, 2010). Others have cautioned against the over-emphasis of any one theoretical perspective, arguing that this can cause practitioners to over-look relationship types and opportunities that are not addressed by that partic-ular approach (Degotardi and Pearson, 2009).

At a time when the number of infants and toddlers in early childhood ser-vices continues to grow, and the focus on relationships between educators, families and communities grows ever stronger, such ambiguities and ideas need to be re-examined and responses sought that do justice to the new reality of children's lives in contemporary society. Encouragingly, there are impor-tant existing and emerging conceptual bases that can be drawn on to under-stand more deeply the relationship worlds of infants and toddlers. In recent years, a growing range of theoretical approaches has been used to investigate both the roles and responsibilities of an infant–toddler educator as well as the characteristics and significance of different relationships within infant–toddler early childhood programmes (e.g. Johansson and White, 2011; Harrison and Sumsion, in press). While infant–toddler professional and research litera-ture continues to be overshadowed by that related to the teaching and learning of older children, this emerging body of knowledge has the potential to enhance professional practice by providing educators with new lenses through which to examine the relationships that develop within early years settings.

Multiple relationships: contexts, networks and perspectives

Overwhelmingly, studies of relationships have emphasized the need for infants to develop a secure, positive relationship with at least one significant other person in their life. In the past, strong arguments were advanced that this rela-tionship needed to be relatively exclusive, with a particular primacy placed on the mother–infant relationship (Degotardi and Pearson, 2009). It is sometimes proposed that any moves to disrupt this bond would be damaging to the mother–infant relationship and, ultimately, the infant. While the significance of the mother–child relationship retains an enduring impact in both societal and early childhood thinking, contemporary approaches have cast the net wider in order to demonstrate that:

- infants and toddlers can form positive and beneficial relationships with multiple caregivers, from both within and outside their immediate family group (Lewis, 2005)
- these relationships differ in characteristics and intensity (Thompson, 2005)

- infants and toddlers also develop relationships with other children, which differ in style from those held with adults (e.g. Wittmer, 2008; Howes, 2009).

Together, these arguments demonstrate that the relationship worlds of infants and toddlers comprise many types of interpersonal connections, all of which have the potential to play a significant role in the child's life, and which may contribute to the child's learning in unique and context-specific ways. They also demonstrate the capabilities of very young children to form, maintain and benefit from relationships with multiple individuals and groups, thus moving thinking away from a strictly exclusive and dyadic conceptualization of relationships.

This shift in thinking is needed because formal infant–toddler education and care contexts have features that clearly differentiate them from most home environments. As group contexts, early childhood programmes include the presence of multiple adults and children. The educators in the setting have particular roles, responsibilities and practices that are different from those of children's parents and family members, and may come and go in ways that family members do not. The setting is designed to cater for groups of similar-aged children who spend periods of time together in the presence of these adults in a designated space. The programme includes activities, experiences and routines that are designed to suit this group-care context, and that are likely to vary from the activities in the home.

When considering how to foster relationships in infant–toddler pro-grammes it is essential to take these specific features into account. Every context, and the individuals and groups within that context, will have sets of practices, priorities and belief systems that will affect the relationship opportunities and experiences that are available to those in that setting. As Mamali (1996, p. 217) explains:

> Interpersonal relationships and communication are always developed in a specific cultural context that has its own values, norms and even institutions to cope with different types and levels of interpersonal relationships.

Mamali draws attention to the context-specific nature of the relationships that occur in any setting, as well as the characteristics of those relationships. Just as cross-cultural variation exists in regards to forms and features of interpersonal relationships (Gudykunst *et al.*, 1996; Kâğıtçıbaşı, 2007), varia-tion also exists in different settings within any one culture. Any understanding of relationships therefore must be firmly founded on an acknowledgement of the attributes of that setting that differentiate it from others. In this way, meaningful relationship-building opportunities and processes can be identified and, ultimately, enhanced in that particular setting.

A growing acceptance of the presence of multiple relationships in the lives of infants and toddlers has seen the recognition that each relationship occurs within a network of other relationships. By virtue of their participation in the centre, infants and toddlers experience relationships with their educators, their peers, their own and other children's parents, as well as relationships between their educators and parents. Each one of these relationships is likely to affect the quality of the others in this relationship network, as any experiences within one relationship context impact on the ways in which relationships are experienced and interpreted in another (Lewis, 2005; Goouch and Powell, 2013). As a result of working with infant-room practitioners to theorize the nature of relationships in their programmes, Goouch and Powell (2013, pp. 51–52) found that many individual and contextual factors came into play in determining the dynamics of any one relationship, as well as the broader relationship network itself. Relationships, they claim, are:

- influenced by the ongoing or changing presence of others in the immediate social context – who comes, stays, visits or leaves
- interconnected – with experiences or characteristics of one relationship having a ripple effect across the entire relationship network
- highly specific and multi-directional – depending on a dynamic interplay of personalities, learning styles, needs and so on
- influenced by the way in which educators, parents and children are positioned by the other people in the context.

Significantly, Goouch and Powell found that it was not just the characteristics of the relationships that mattered, but also the ways in which all involved *thought about* those relationships. When reflecting on the role that they played in the relationships in their programme, educators not only drew on perspectives from theory, but also on their own relationship experiences, past, present, personal and professional. Parents came to the centre with their own relationship history and experiences, as well as expectations about the programme and role of the educators within that setting. All of these different perspectives were located within the philosophical and managerial context of the centre, as well as in wider societal discourses about early childhood education and care.

To return to Hinde's (1997) original assertion, it is indeed the case that relationships within infant–toddler early childhood and care programmes are complicated! It is for this reason that development of a comprehensive understanding of the many different relationships that make up infants' and toddlers' relationship worlds in early childhood education and care settings necessitates the casting of a wide theoretical net. A professional knowledge base about relationships needs to include contemporary evidence from research that can shed light on the characteristics of the multiple relationships that occur in that setting. It also needs to locate those relationships in the real-world context as experienced by the children, the educators and parents. What kinds of relationship do educators and parents want for their children? What value do they attribute to any particular type of relationship? What do they notice and what do they encourage? And how do infants and toddlers themselves experience the relationships in which they are immersed? Answers to these questions can help researchers and educators alike to appreciate the social situatedness of relationships, and locate the nature and value of any one relationship within the wider relationship network that makes up infant and toddler relationship worlds. By combining perspectives from research and practice, we have the potential to understand both the theoretical and the real-world significance of infants' and toddlers' relationship worlds for all involved.

About this book

We have written this book with a wide readership in mind that includes undergraduate and postgraduate students of early childhood education and care, as well as professional early childhood practitioners and researchers. While much of the text refers to theory and practice in early childhood education, we acknowledge the range of professionals and practitioners whose work is so critical in supporting the growth and development of infants and toddlers, and trust that the content presented here will be of interest to this wider audience. Our rationale in writing this book is that the development and implementation of effective relationship-based early education and care programmes is reliant on a detailed understanding of the various kinds of relationship that are desired and experienced by young children, their families and educators. Educators can then be open to the kinds of relationship that they have the potential to foster in their programmes, and the significance of these different relationships for those involved. Through an appreciation of the richness and complexity of the relationship worlds of infant–toddler programmes, all involved can invest in the types of relationship that will benefit the learning, development and lived experiences of those participating in that programme.

The book is founded on a number of research projects conducted by the two authors, each of which investigated different aspects of the relationships that occurred in infant–toddler programmes. In Chapter 2, we set the scene for the ways in which we will approach the topic of relationships by explaining the contribution to be gained from a multi-perspectival approach to this topic. The four subsequent chapters present data generated in these different projects in order to explore:

- different dimensions and functions of relationships
- forming relationships

- relationships with and between adults
- relationships with peers.

In each of these chapters, the authors bring their own unique perspectives to the topic and the data that they present. In these chapters, 'Research in focus' boxes are used to identify the study from which the data was derived, and provide a brief summary of the context and method of that study. We use this format below to introduce the authors and their interests, as well as the studies that you will be reading about as you progress through the book.

Research in focus: introducing the authors and their research

The authors
Sheila Degotardi is an early childhood teacher, lecturer and researcher who has, over the past 15 years, researched different aspects of infants' relatedness and relationships with significant others. Her work has focused strongly on different elements and contributors to the interpersonal connections that occur between educators, infants and their peers in infant–toddler early childhood education and care programmes. She has combined observation, interview and survey-based data to attempt to understand relatedness and relationships from a number of theoretical and real-world perspectives.

Emma Pearson has engaged in various aspects of social and cultural diversity through her teaching, research and engagement in community outreach over the past two decades. In her work, she is committed to understanding and promoting the importance of diverse belief and value systems in early childhood theory, policy and practice. Her research is focused on understanding diverse beliefs parental beliefs about and priorities for young children. In this work, she has benefited significantly from the insights and experiences offered by opportunities to work with many colleagues from different parts of the world, including North Korea and Vanuatu.

The focus research
The research to be presented throughout this book is derived from the following studies.

Relationship Perspectives involved a number of explorations of parent and educator perspectives on the form and function of relationships experienced by infants and toddlers in early childhood centres. The data comprised, in the first stage, an online survey distributed to childcare centres across New South Wales. The second stage of data collection involved a case-study observation of the interpersonal relatedness of infants and toddlers in one early childhood classroom, and drew on interviews with educators and parents to interpret the significance of their relationships. This stage of the study also involved parent and educator focus groups, which followed up on key results from stage one and also gave participants an opportunity to share their own ideas and experiences of forming relationships in formal infant and toddler settings. Data from these various aspects of the *Relationship Perspectives* study are referred to in Chapters 3, 5 and 6, and can also be found in Degotardi, Sweller and Pearson (2013) and Degotardi (2014).

Making Connections: The Dynamics of Relationship Formation was a three-month study of three infants, their parents and educators as these three infants transitioned into an early childhood infant room. The data comprised close, video-recorded observations of the infants across a three-month period during which their educators and parents were interviewed at several points during the transition about the processes which they felt were influencing the relationships that these infants were developing over time. Data from the *Making Connections: The Dynamics of Relationship Formation* study form the basis for our discussion in Chapter 4, and can be found in Degotardi and Pearson (2010), Degotardi (2011a, 2011b, 2013, 2014) and Pearson (2011).

Understanding Infants was a study investigating the ways that infant educators interpreted the behaviours of infants in their programme, and the implications that these interpretations had for their interactions with these infants. Educators were video-recorded during their play and routine interactions with infants, and were then asked to discuss the infants' actions when they reviewed the recording. Data from the *Understanding Infants* study are presented and interpreted in Chapter 5, and revisited in our concluding chapter; further findings from this study can be found in Degotardi and Davis (2008), Degotardi (2010, 2013), and Degotardi and Sweller (2012).

Each of the chapters situates the research data within a wider discussion of contemporary approaches to understanding relationships, comparing and contrasting our own theoretical approaches with those that have been applied in various disciplines to understand the nature and significance of relationships. While we draw on a wide range of research from many countries, we should emphasize that our research, which we present and interpret in many of the chapters, was conducted in Australia. The excerpts that are included therefore need to be considered in light of Australian institutional, social and cultural contexts.

Our aim in this book is to highlight diversity by introducing the reader to a wide range of theoretical, practice and community-based views on relationships. These should not be seen as fully addressing the many complex issues surrounding social and cultural difference and similarity across diverse contexts, but rather serve to prompt readers to engage in and think about the unique features of relationships within any given place and time. We do this so that those with vested interests in supporting relationships in these education and care settings can consider a diversity of views in order to understand the intricacies of infants' and toddlers' relationship worlds. By adopting a 'research into practice' approach, we also hope to provide a means for educators to reflect on their own practice and context in order to make informed, and inclusive, professional decisions about how to support caring, teaching and learning through relationships in their own context.

Notes

1   In this book, we use the word 'infant' to refer to babies and young children aged 0 to 24 months. The word 'toddler' is used to refer to older, 'toddling' infants and young children aged up to 36 months. There is therefore a degree of overlap in ages between infants and toddlers.

2   Across different countries, a range of terms is used to refer to people who are employed to care for and educate young children. As qualification requirements vary within early childhood centres, as well as within and between countries, we have chosen to use the word 'educator' as an all-encompassing term to refer to those who work in a professional capacity with young children. The word 'teacher', when used, refers to an educator who has a university-level early childhood qualification.

2 Multiple perspectives: images, evidence and professional practice

The early childhood field embodies a rich diversity of perspectives. At its core, it combines a keen respect for knowledge and a deep passion to make a difference in the lives of young children and their parents.

Jack Shonkoff

In Chapter 1, we proposed that a wealth of different theoretical and stakeholder perspectives contribute towards the ways in which we perceive and understand young children's relationships. In this second introductory chapter, we detour briefly from our focus on relationships to discuss the topic of multiple perspectives in more detail. We situate our discussion firmly within the context of early childhood professional practice, explaining how each different perspective constitutes a knowledge base that has the potential to influence the way in which educators approach their daily work with young children and their families. We begin with a discussion of the infant–toddler context by examining some traditional societal and theoretical forces that have influenced, and continue to influence, infant–toddler education. In the context of increasing calls for early childhood education to be more 'evidence based', we explore the meaning of this term by asking what should count as evidence, as well as how can this evidence be used effectively in programmes that cater for diverse populations of young children, their families and educators? If, as Shonkoff (2006, p. xi) argues, the early childhood field is to 'make a difference in the lives of young children and their parents', an important place to start is with an examination of the knowledge bases that are available, as well as the ways in which these knowledge bases can be used to enhance professional practice.

Sites of struggle

In recent times, the early childhood field has seen a dramatic increase in awareness of the foundational importance of children's first years of life. Early childhood educators now have greater access than ever before to an expansive body of evidence that demonstrates the significance of early experiences for children's development, learning and wellbeing. At the same time, a focus on establishing and building professional capacity and professionalism in the early childhood field has been accompanied by the need to consider carefully how (and whether) such evidence is used to inform practice and the source of valid and valuable evidence (Urban, 2010). Shonkoff (2006) rightly states that there are many perspectives available to those working with young children and families, some of which complement one another and some of which may challenge or directly conflict with current ways of thinking and working. Questions of 'which evidence?' and 'whose perspective?' regularly come to the fore as early childhood educators grapple with decisions about how best to enhance the lives, learning and development of the young children and their families who attend their programmes.

Many educators now work in a context where they have more access to ideas about what constitutes, and how to deliver, effective early childhood practice than at any time in history. However, the availability of such a broad knowledge base has its problems. Tensions arise as educators and their employers try to reconcile conflicting messages from theory, research, policy, regulatory bodies, families, societies and their own experience about how things should be done and how they should conduct their work with children and families. Professionalism is bound up with multiple discourses about expert knowledge and skills, educator responsibility, performance and autonomy, and professional status (Fenech, Sumsion and Shepherd, 2010). It is understood that 'being professional' involves the constant negotiation of a number of societal, theoretical and political forces, as educators strive to do their job well at a time when perspectives abound about what it means to be an early childhood educator and what is regarded as 'good' practice (Woodrow, 2008; Bradbury, 2012). What is clear is that the 'debate about teachers and their 'professionalism' is ongoing, complex and dependent on circumstances' (Bradbury, 2012, p. 183). Uncertainties and struggles are inevitable, yet these uncertainties can themselves bring about an enhanced sense of professionalism. As Sachs (2003) argues, professionalism is 'a site of struggle between various interest groups' (p. 121), and therefore it is by coming to grips with, and critically reflecting on, these multiple discourses that educators can construct the kinds of professional wisdom and judgement that can boost the competence of, and their confidence in, their day-to-day practice.

Some forces at play

All professions are embedded in a complex web of forces that exert a strong influence on the priorities of that profession, on the roles that are established and the day-to-day practices that are played out. The field of infant–toddler education is no exception. Sims and Hutchins (2011) acknowledge the power of these ideological forces when they acknowledge that, throughout its history, infant–toddler education has been subject to controversy and debate about what characterizes positive and beneficial early experiences for these young children. Such forces raise questions such as:

- Why or when should infants and toddlers attend early years settings?
- Who should be responsible for their care and education?
- What constitutes the best kinds of experience for this age group?
- How do infants and toddlers learn and develop, and what role do educators play in this process?

These forces are often entrenched and 'unspoken', so can exert considerable influence without educators' conscious acknowledgement. The challenge is to confront and examine these forces because:

> When caregivers understand the different cultural blueprints that are operating they are better able to bridge the divide between different and sometime conflicting belief systems.
>
> (Sims and Hutchins, 2011, p. xxxvi)

Recognition of the existence of these forces is evidently one of the first steps towards the conscious awareness and deliberation of the complex knowledge bases that underpin infant–toddler education understanding. We therefore begin our examination of perspectives by critiquing two significant forces: images of educators and images of children.

Images of educators

Images of educators are shaped by a series of contextually based perspectives on what is meant by an 'early childhood educator'; what obligations and aspirations educators have in regards to young children and their families; and what types of personal and professional characteristics are regarded as important, and by whom? Most educators have a professional identity, made up in part by the personal qualities, attitudes, roles and practices that have personal and societal value. As Manning-Morton (2006) points out, teaching and its associated professional identity is value-laden, and prone to be influenced by predominant *images* or belief systems about what constitutes an 'ideal' early childhood educator. These belief systems will result in the prioritizing of certain types of expertise and practice over others, and thus will influence the nature of the educational programme in terms of both what is taught and how it is taught. Below, we identify some traditional conceptualizations of infant–toddler education and caregiving practice, and review some of the ways that these images have been discussed in more contemporary literature.

The mother–educator

The ideology of motherhood and mothering is perhaps one of the most pervasive forces to influence infant–toddler education. Ailwood (2008) argues that this ideology, which has come to characterize early childhood education in general, stems from the belief that 'mothers are the single most important carers of their children and that this relationship must be defended at any cost' (p. 157). Such beliefs have given rise, in part, to questions of whether infant and toddler programmes are detrimental to children. The strongest proponents of this argument came from the realm of attachment theory, based on Bowlby's (1958) claim that infants could suffer from 'maternal deprivation' if they were placed for any amount of time in settings away from their mother. Current debates surrounding the provision of paid maternity leave lend support to the idea that infant care is best placed at home with mothers, and thus cut to the core of questions about who should best care for infants.

In some instances, motherhood ideologies position infant–toddler educators as a 'necessary evil' who provide care for young children whose mothers need or choose to work. This positioning links provision of care to economic growth, as well as to the rights of mothers and children to have access to high-quality services (May, 2007). It is not surprising that those working in infant–toddler education and care are often caught up in discourses of mothering, where educators are often viewed as mother-substitutes who ideally should embody the characteristics and priorities of 'good' mothers (Canella, 1997). In many countries, the idea that caring for infants and toddlers is a natural, maternal quality is reflected in the lower levels of, and requirements for, qualified staff in programmes for under–2s (Ireland, 2006; Rockel, 2009; Clark and Baylis, 2012). The predominant focus in the early childhood relationship literature on one-to-one infant–educator interactions as a basis of high-quality care can be regarded as a further manifestation of the mothering ideology. Although such interactions are undoubtedly important, critics have argued that they do not sufficiently take into consideration the unique characteristics of group early years settings, such as the presence of multiple children and adults, and the opportunities that the group settings therefore afford (Shpancer, 2002; Lewis, 2005; Degotardi and Pearson, 2009).

While it is often assumed that the care of young children has traditionally been the primary responsibility of mothers, it is also important to recognize that this may, in fact, not represent the reality of many young children's lives. McHale (2007) describes how many infants are now co-parented, with both mother and father taking active roles in parenting. Caregiving and child-rearing, he argues, should not be regarded as a predominantly maternal characteristic as the role is frequently undertaken by both males and females. McHale also challenges the idea that infants and toddlers are best cared for by only one key adult. He extends his discussion of co-parenting to include co-caregiving, thus calling for a recognition that the care and raising of infants is often shared with members of the extended family, friends and community members (Kâğitçibaşi, 2007).

The carer–educator

One of the most debated tensions in early childhood education revolves around notions of care and education, and the relationship between the two. Rockel (2009) has explored this controversial topic to consider its historical roots and its contemporary influence in infant–toddler pedagogy. At its most basic, she explains, the concept of 'caring for' denotes the supervision of young children while their parents are elsewhere, thus conceptualizing educators as child-minders or baby-sitters. 'Caring for' also relates to the provision of physical care, closely associated with the historical practice of employing mothercraft nurses and 'matrons' in infant–toddler rooms as 'caregivers' who monitored and ensured the health and hygiene of 0–2-year-old children (May, 2007). Rockel (2009) argues that the pervasive divide between care and education devalues the work of infant–toddler educators by equating any sense of professional expertise to intuition or simply being 'good with babies' (p. 4). On the one hand, this can contribute to the perceived low status of infant–toddler educators, both by those working in the field as well as those in the community at large. On the other hand, it can bring about pedagogical tensions as educators try to find a balance between routine, care-related and play- or exploration-based experiences in their curriculum (Degotardi, Semann and Shepherd, 2012).

Taggart (2011) argues strongly that the early childhood field needs to move on from this relentless separation of care and education, claiming that the continued debate reflects 'the persistence of an outdated equation between caring and female irrationality or anti-intellectualism' (p. 85). He calls for educators to reclaim the care aspect as an integral aspect of their professional responsibility towards young children and their families. An example of this can be found in Manning-Morton's (2006) consideration of physical care, during which she details recent evidence on the significance of touch for emotional wellbeing and self-identity. Physical care, she argues, provides essential tactile and touch experiences as well as opportunities for the kinds of close, responsive interactions that form the basis of trusting and supportive relationships. Brooker (2009) further extends the concept of care by proposing that a caring relationship is an ethical one that encompasses the ways that infants and their caregivers communicate and respond to one another's intentions, feelings and ideas. In this way, care is not simply something that is provided *by* adults *for* infants, but is a psychological aspect of the social environment that is co-constructed through respectful and reciprocal interactions. These ethical and pedagogical concepts of care extend on the traditional notions of supervision and physical care, and have the potential to contribute significantly towards the professional status of those working with the youngest children.

The interventionist–educator

The significance of early childhood education and care programmes is often justified by reference to the argument that they provide valuable opportunities to address disadvantage and provide intervention for vulnerable children and their families. Wong (2007) draws on nationalistic and economic discourses to explain how the early childhood field has a long history of regarding early education as a means to increase workforce participation, enhance children's potential and reduce risks of future social disadvantage and participation in antisocial activity. Historically, in many countries, orphanages or crèches were established to protect infants from 'incompetent' or 'immoral' mothers (May, 2007). Many early childhood organizations were originally established as philanthropic organizations that aimed to assist mothers in need, and 'save' poor children from their disadvantaged and impoverished circumstances.

The interventionist approach can be seen today in the use of evidence about the significance of children's first years of life to argue for increased resources for the 0–3 sector. Cheeseman (2007) identifies brain research findings that young children are highly influenced, or even 'moulded' (p. 245), by early experiences, as one of the underpinnings of many social welfare programmes as well as concerted efforts to support the development of high-quality early childhood programmes. While such moves can certainly have the positive effect of enhancing the lives and potential of all children, if the emphasis is solely on ameliorating the effects of disadvantage, this discourse has the potential to portray mothers as needy or selfish, and position children as vulnerable and in need of societal protection (Cheeseman, 2007; Wong, 2007). Educators are in danger of being regarded as 'saviours', 'do-gooders' or 'experts', who can seek out and 'treat' potential problems in children or families when, or even before, they arise (Urban, 2010).

Images of children

Every person holds particular ideas about the nature and learning of children; ideas that are, at least in part, constructed through individual history, societal discourses and cultural belief systems. Rinaldi highlights the power of these images for educators:

> . . . there are many possible images. Some focus on what children are, what they have, and what they can do, while others, unfortunately, focus on what children are not, do not have, and what they are not

able to do. . . the image is a cultural convention, a cultural interpretation and therefore a political and social issue, which enables you to
recognize or not to recognize certain qualities and potential of
children.

(Rinaldi, 2001, p. 50)

Lally (2006) describes educators' images of children as an organizing theory,
which greatly influences what they notice and the ways in which they interpret
infants' actions and expressions. Images of infants are closely bound to particular conceptualizations of educators, as early childhood practitioners draw on
these images to determine what they regard as the appropriate means to
respond to what they see.

The incapable infant

Lally (2006) claims that 'Many people look at infants and do not see anything
but an eating, sleeping, and defecating machine' (p. 11), and, in doing so,
argues that the perceived relative youth and immaturity of very young children results in a view of these children as the 'early unformed' (p. 11). Clark
and Baylis (2012) agree that the capabilities of infants are often overlooked by
both educators and society at large, and contend that the pervasive emphasis of society on the physical care of very young children portrays them as
incapable, powerless and passive recipients of care. Not only does this image
constrain any kind of agency on the part of the infant, but by neglecting to
recognize the intellectual and social capabilities of infants and toddlers, it
severely limits the kinds of experiences that are offered to them. There appears
to be little point in talking to a baby who is believed incapable of understanding,
or in providing quality, stimulating materials for a baby who is thought to
register little awareness of the outside world.

The vulnerable infant

While many would now challenge the negative view of infancy portrayed by
extreme versions of the 'incapable' infant, others argue that a delicate balance
needs to be found between recognizing infant capabilities and acknowledging
the vulnerability that is associated with the infancy period. White (2011) writes
that 'it is risky to oversize the child's competence or undersize their vulnerability' (p. 186) and, in doing so, highlights the fact that, because of their relative
immaturity, infants are highly dependent on others to meet their physical,
social and intellectual needs. This does place them in a position of vulnerability, so educators are in an ethical position to ensure that these young children are protected and nurtured. Yet when the vulnerabilities of infants and
toddlers become the dominant consideration, educators risk adopting a protective stance towards infants and toddlers, therefore limiting vital opportunities
to explore and interact with their material and social world. By becoming

overly protective, there is a danger that educators can fall into a 'rescuing' role where young children's learning is limited as they are prevented from solving problems, taking risks and experiencing consequences (Gonzalez-Mena and Widmeyer Eyer, 2007).

The invisible infant

While the body of literature about the learning, development, education and care of infants and toddlers is growing, this age group remains one of the most under-represented in both early childhood research and professional literature (Berthelsen, 2010). Educators working with infants and toddlers have expressed concern about the lack of professional literature and professional/development opportunities in the field, expressing the view that this absence brings about a feeling of invisibility, not only of the children, but of those working with this age group (Clark and Baylis, 2012).

This invisibility extends to policy documents, where some countries have opted for a holistic curriculum approach rather than one that distinguishes between children of different age groups. In the UK, the Birth to Three Matters Framework (Department for Education and Skills, 2002), which was introduced as a means of addressing a lack of reference to the first three years in early childhood policy documents, was superseded by the Early Years Foundation Stage (Department for Education and Skills, 2007). This new framework focused broadly on the learning and learning outcomes of the whole early childhood age range, a move that Nutbrown and Page (2008) link to a feeling of marginalization in those working with younger children. Similarly, in Australia, the introduction of the national early childhood curriculum document – the Early Years Learning Framework – openly rejects terms such as 'infant' and 'toddler', instead opting to use the words 'child' or 'children' as all-encompassing terms (Australian Department of Education, Employment and Workplace Relations, 2009). While justifying their choice on a desire to focus on capabilities, rather than vulnerabilities, and to avoid portraying any age group as an 'other', some of the authors themselves acknowledge that only time will tell whether this omission may be a point of tension in educators' interpretation and use of the policy document (Sumsion et al., 2009).

Thoughtful agents

While it is impossible to be impervious to images such as those detailed above, an increasing focus on the professionalization of early childhood educators requires a careful consideration of a more contemporary and evidence-informed knowledge base than that afforded by traditional conceptualizations of educators and children. A central aspect of this move is the call for educators to become 'thoughtful agents' (Clark and Baylis, 2012, p. 133) who explore and challenge entrenched views in order to moderate their influence through the consideration of contemporary theoretical approaches to infant–toddler education and care.

While there is no single definition of 'professionalism' as it applies to early childhood practice, a common characteristic is the acquisition, then ongoing reflective construction and re-construction, of a specialized knowledge base upon which to ground practice (Dalli, 2008). The advocacy for professionalism is linked closely to a global desire to increase both the quantity and quality of early childhood programmes (Urban, 2010). When paired with the reality of increasing numbers of young children attending early years settings, a widespread acknowledgement of the critical period of early childhood has led to the belief that the early years workforce 'has to be professionalized in order to meet the increasingly challenging requirements of the work' (Urban, 2010, p. 179). Knowledge, argues Urban, 'and the way it is produced, distributed and applied' (p. 181), is central to the professional system.

Accordingly, educators and policy-makers are often called on to ensure that early childhood pedagogy is *evidence-based* in order to enhance the quality and outcomes associated with early childhood programmes (Biesta, 2007). According to Buysse, Wesley, Snyder and Winton (2006), 'the words evidence-based practice have become part of our everyday vocabulary in the early childhood field' (p. 2). In the next section, we therefore discuss what is meant by 'evidence-based practice', including what kinds of evidence should count in conceptualizations of professional early years practice and how such evidence can support and contribute to the day-to-day practice of infant–toddler educators.

Evidence-based practice

In some circles, the term 'evidence-based practice' has become synonymous with the use of scientific evidence to support practice (Biesta, 2007; Fox, 2011). In the extreme, research evidence is argued to hold the answers to practice-based problems through the generation of scientifically defendable knowledge about effective, 'best' practice. According to Biesta (2007), 'there is a strong push for experimental research that, according to proponents of evidence-based education, is the only method capable of providing secure evidence about "what works"' (p. 3). This top-down conceptualization of evidence is often translated into lists of recommended practices or practice-based scripts that, if followed, are expected to bring about efficacious results.

'Evidence-based practice', however, is defined quite differently by Buysse and Wesley (2006a). Their concept of evidence-based practice involves a recognition and integration of knowledge and perspectives from science, practice and policy with the aim of closing the gap between research-derived knowledge and early childhood practice. Evidence-based practice is not a prescriptive set of guidelines or recommendations that aim to create high-quality practice, but instead is 'a decision-making process that integrates the best available research evidence with family and professional wisdom and values' that are unique to a specific context (Buysse and Wesley, 2006b, p. xiv). It is based on the premise that professional educators should consider broad sources of evidence, and thus construct and consult a specialized knowledge base in order to make sound and justifiable, appropriate decisions about how best to support the particular group of children and families using their services.

What counts as evidence?

Recently, one of us argued that 'the complexities of infant–toddler pedagogy can only be addressed by increasing the professional knowledge base of those working in the field' (Degotardi, 2011c, p. 3). Research findings constitute an essential component of this knowledge base on which educators justify their practice. Research evidence challenges educators to understand different perspectives, providing them with tools to challenge current ways of thinking and acting, the result of which are educators who are 'more secure and more open to self-reflection in the light of more knowledge' (Page, Clare and Nutbrown, 2013, p. 14).

While research evidence about the significance of the first three years of life continues to grow, it is notable that much of this evidence is derived from studies in the home, or experimental studies that are far removed from the everyday lives of educators, children and families in early childhood services (Johansson, 2011). Accordingly, Berthelsen (2010) points to the 'youthfulness' (p. 83) of research about birth-to-3 programmes and calls for the development of a stronger research culture if questions relating to what it is like to be, to learn and to teach in these programmes are to be explored. Recent years have seen an increase in such research, with the publication of several infant–toddler specialized books and special issues (e.g. Johansson and White, 2011; Rayna and Laevers, 2011; Oberhuemer, 2012), and increasing numbers of professional publications have communicated relevant research findings to a wide educator readership (e.g. Wittmer and Petersen, 2009; Sims and Hutchins, 2011; Page *et al.*, 2013). However, infant–toddler research continues to be under-represented to date, so there remains a need to ensure that the interests, needs and capabilities of our youngest children, their educators and families are made more visible in both research and professional literature.

Boundaries exist, though, between the worlds of researchers and practitioners, and these boundaries challenge the assumption that early childhood research will automatically support and enhance practice. Buysse and Wesley (2006a) acknowledge the age-old tension between research and practice by asking 'Why won't practitioners do what the research says? Why don't researchers study what really matters in practice?' (p. 3). They acknowledge the challenge of translating research findings into an accessible form that is both available to a wide and diverse educator audience *and* applicable to the local contexts in which they work. While Shonkoff (2010) espoused an imperative for researchers to disseminate their findings in professional literature and policy documents, the reality remains that the ways in which different people interpret and draw implications from such documents will depend on more than exposure to research evidence alone. Evidence-based practice *is not* synonymous with synopses of best-available research evidence; the latter comprising collections or summaries of empirical evidence which, if regarded by educators as having little relation or relevance to their own daily practice, is in danger of being rejected (Biesta, 2007).

Researchers and educators currently belong to very different communities of practice, and their priorities and agendas are therefore very different. For this reason, Berthelsen (2010) acknowledges that 'much of the knowledge that is generated by research is a moving target and this is a challenge for practitioners' (p. 84). Researchers seek out and generate knowledge over time, building and testing theories and models with the aim of constructing models to conceptualize and explain particular phenomena. They concentrate, according to Shonkoff (2006), on *'what we don't know'* (p. vii, original italics), on explaining the unexplained and filling current knowledge gaps. In contrast, the focus of educators is on the pragmatic, day-to-day effectiveness of what they do. They are often called on to respond immediately to issues, with the primary consideration being *'what we should do'* (p. vii). Educators therefore need to draw on a knowledge base that includes, but also extends beyond, research evidence.

For reasons such as these, Buysse and Wesley (2006a) argue that successful, professional decision-making should not only be based on empirically sound evidence, but also on contextually relevant knowledge, learning and values of key stakeholders. Their argument is consistent with Pearson's (2011) view that the research evidence available to many early childhood educators working around the world is insufficient to account for the diverisity in relationship perspectives that we argue is central to understanding the relationship worlds of infants. Both of these standpoints recognize the need for educators and policy-makers to identify, interpret and evaluate a range of perspectives when needing to solve practice problems or address complex social issues. In this way, the dynamic process of evidence-based practice tunes in to the diversity and uncertainty of the early childhood field, and the complexity of working with a range of different perspectives is recognized and used to the benefit of young children and families (Shonkoff, 2006).

Practice-based evidence

Buysse and Wesley (2006a) advocate for the incorporation of collective and individual wisdoms, values, belief structures and experiences into the professional knowledge base and in doing so, recognize that there is valuable evidence to be drawn from key stakeholders in early childhood programmes. They contend that professional decision-making should involve an integration of research evidence with the knowledge gained from practitioner experience in a local context. By broadening the evidence base, educators are able to weigh up the value and relevance of each piece of evidence in order to make decisions that are contextually relevant. Educators themselves become directly involved in the generation of professional knowledge, as do the families that use their programmes. The term *'practice-based evidence'* is used to recognize the validity of knowledge that is derived through the experiences of key stakeholders (Biesta, 2007; Urban, 2010; Fox, 2011). Practice-based evidence includes:

- knowledge derived from particular educational approaches, which may be based more on a philosophical belief than on empirical research findings (Buysse and Wesley, 2006a)
- 'craft knowledge' (Winton, 2006) and 'funds of knowledge' (Hedges, 2012), which consist of insights about the practicalities and moralities related to the real-world experience of delivering early childhood programmes within a specific community (Biesta, 2007)
- the perspectives, knowledge and values of educators and the populations that they serve.

In this way, the characteristics of individual children, families, local contexts, and broader societal beliefs and discourses are integrated into professional decision-making processes (Buysse and Wesley, 2006a). The use of a broad evidence base allows for judgements to be made about 'the most appropriate course of actions in the specific circumstances in a context of informal rules, heuristics, norms and values' (Sanderson, 2003, cited in Biesta, 2007, p. 10). The concept of evidence-based practice therefore shifts from focusing on individual decision-making, based on traditional ideologies or evidence acquired from decontextualized sources, to an emphasis on the establishment and sharing of collective knowledge bases through the critical consideration of multiple perspectives (Urban, 2010).

The significance of critical reflection

When conceptualized as a blend of research-based and practice-based knowledge, evidence-based practice is able to bridge the gap between theory and practice, as the process provides educators with a tool to determine how and when to adopt, adapt and apply the findings from theoretically derived sources to their local context. Educators adopt a researcher stance themselves, by generating and considering practice-based evidence alongside that provided from empirical sources. This move, according to Urban (2010, p. 183), situates educators as evidence-gatherers, as 'key actors, not recipients, in the professional system' (p. 183), and provides them with the professional identity and integrity to make meaningful changes to their practice.

But evidence, by itself, is not enough to bring about change. Urban (2008) characterizes early childhood practice as a practice of uncertainties and competing possibilities, which 'elude any simplistic *problem-solving-through-application-of knowledge* mechanism' (p. 144, original italics). What is needed is an ability and willingness to be a critical and reflective consumer of evidence. Professionalism is thus linked to the process of reflective practice through which it is possible to consider and weigh up multiple sources of evidence in order to make informed decisions about practice. Appleby described this process as follows:

> Reflective practice as an integral part of professional identity develops most effectively within a culture or learning community where individuals are actively listening and responding to the thoughts and experience of others.
>
> (Appleby 2010, p. 10)

Some final thoughts

Given the range of perspectives on children and early childhood (some of them quite contentious) presented in this chapter, it seems most realistic to view professionalism as reflecting an ability to think critically about multiple perspectives from multiple sources. Moss (2006) sums up the professional knowledge that is derived from this process as 'perspectival, partial, and provisional' (p. 36). Perspectival because it is reflective of the views from which it has been constructed, partial and provisional because it is always evolving, being subject to influence from new perspectives as they arise.

We would argue that professionalism should, in itself, constitute a relationship-based process, requiring the reciprocal exchange, negotiation and debate of various types of evidence between researchers, practitioners and families. This view of professional practice is reflected in Dalli's (2008) New Zealand study of teachers' understandings of professionalism in which the idea of collaborative relationships was regarded as a major component. The teachers in Dalli's research recognized the importance of the development of specialized knowledge and of working together, caring, listening and engaging in respectful dialogue with other educators, parents, management and community members at large. In this way, knowing and acting become 'two sides of the same coin' (Urban and Dalli, 2012, p. 158) and professional knowledge and actions are collaboratively constructed through a process of critical inquiry where multiple sources of evidence are used to transform practice in locally relevant ways.

As the title of this book suggests, our focus is on highlighting 'multiplicity' in perspectives, as it relates not only to research but also to policies, practice and individual priorities. Our contention, supported by the evidence that we draw on throughout the book, is that effective relationship-building in formal early childhood settings requires engagement with these multiple perspectives. The deeply held values and priorities of early childhood professionals, families, and the range of stakeholders that influence policy and practice, all have a crucial role to play in shaping young children's early relationship experiences. In Chapter 3, we highlight some of these priorities, through reference to excerpts from our own work with children, families and professionals.

3 What kind of relationship? Variations in dimensions and functions

People interweave in a multitude of relationships.
Ann Elisabeth Auhagen and Maria von Salisch

In Chapter 1, we introduced the idea that infants and toddlers are immersed in many different relationships, which extend beyond the home setting to include relationships with adults and peers in early childhood education and care settings. In the introduction to their book on the diversity of human relationships, Auhagen and von Salish (1996) summarize the significance of multiple relationships in people's lives when they write that 'people's everyday lives are not only shaped by "major" relationships . . . they are often filled with a variety of actions and expectations from other relationships' (p. 1). The dynamic nature of everyday human daily existence means that young children, their educators and parents continuously 'weave' in and out of these relationships, relating to different people, engaging in different types of interactions, and fulfilling different goals and needs. This interconnectedness between individuals, social contexts and the meaning associated with everyday functioning prompted Duck (1998) to write that 'Relationships are a part of life, and everyday life is a part of all relationships' (p. 84). In other words, relationships are meaningful, not only because of the inherently social nature of human life but also because they provide a means of fulfilling the goals and intentions that are significant in any given time and place.

What this means is that there are many different kinds of relationships, and that these relationships will differ in terms of the forms that they take and the functions they fulfil. In this chapter, we explore some of these variations. We begin by addressing the topic of relationship dimensions with the aim of exploring particular lines along which the characteristics of relationships can vary. We then identify contributing factors to relationship variation.

The second half of the chapter then draws on data from the *Relationship Perspectives* study to demonstrate the different kinds and functions of relationships reflected in the experiences of two toddlers during a short period of their day in an early childhood centre. The themes introduced in this chapter will be revisited and discussed in more depth through the course of the rest of the book when we explore approaches to understanding relationship formation, relationships with and between adults, and relationships with peers. We also explore the different ways in which the observed relationships can be interpreted, both theoretically and in practice. Returning to the 'sites of struggle' notion presented in Chapter 2, we highlight that contemporary notions of relationship formation rightly acknowledge and embrace complexity in relationships, meaning that highly effective relationships can be established only on the basis of mutual trust, grounded in shared and open understandings of varied relationships priorities and perspectives.

The dimensions of relationships

One way of thinking about relationship variation is through an examination of relationship dimensions. Hinde (1997) identifies a number of different dimensions that can be used to understand why the characteristics associated with one relationship may differ from those of another. Several points of variation can be observed at the level of the interactions.

- Interactions can vary in their *content or topic* as the behaviours and conversations that are typically enacted in one relationship may be very different from those enacted in another.
- Interaction can vary in terms of the *relative frequency* in which these interactions occur.
- Different relationships will also be characterized by different *interactional qualities*, with variation in conversational style and in intensity as well as in the use of non-verbal signals, touch and eye contact.
- Finally, some relationships contain a narrow *range of interactions*, whereas in other relationships, the range and diversity of interactions is much greater.

In some relationships, interactions are typically reciprocal, in that they are characterized by the similarity and mutual engagement of both individuals. Other interactions are complementary, when the interaction style of each person involved differs from that of the partner because each person responds to the different roles and interests of the other. The dimensions of reciprocity vs complementarity highlight the psychological aspect of relationships, as variation will depend not only on who is involved, but also on their knowledge of one another. Levels of intimacy also vary, with psychological attributes such as trust, empathy and openness reliant not only on how well one person knows the other, but also on the shared understandings and expectations about that relationship that have been established over time. Finally, relationships vary according to commitment, or the extent to which each person is willing to afford effort to ensure their maintenance over time. According to Hinde (1997), commitment involves 'incorporating part of the self into the relationship – or the relationship into the self' (p. 269). Commitment therefore comprises a psychological investment, as part of the individual's very sense of self is bound up with their conceptualization of the relationship. If we pause to consider the different relationships we each have across multiple contexts (home, work, extended family, and so on), and the varying levels of investment we put into them, these multiple dimensions come to life.

What contributes to relationship variation?

Duck (1999) identifies three main factors that he claims contribute significantly towards the characteristics of any particular relationship. These factors – as described below – are useful to consider when explaining why relationships, and the interactional behaviours that they involve, can vary along different dimensions.

Interior needs and concerns

All individuals bring thoughts, feelings and motivations to any relationship context. The extent to which a person 'likes' or 'dislikes' any individual will certainly be a driving factor in relationship formation, yet this alone is not sufficient to explain when and why a particular relationship will develop. Humans have needs that are linked to their social circumstances, and therefore will seek to meet those needs through the relationships that they form with others (Weiss, 1974). People's memories and understandings of past and present relationship experiences will also impact on the kinds of relationship they seek and the ways that they conduct those relationships. In addition, a person's desire (or not) for inclusion, company and acceptance is also significant. This dimension highlights why it is important to locate the interior needs and concerns of any individual within a community of others and other relationships.

Exterior factors

Exterior factors comprise features of the person's social and cultural world. Social and cultural groups often hold strong beliefs about acceptable and unacceptable ways of relating to others, and rules about the kinds of relationship that can and cannot be formed within that community. Specific communities have a vested interest in fostering the kinds of relationship that they believe will serve the needs, goals and priorities of that community.

The relationships, for example, that are deemed suitable in an adult-only workplace will not be the same as those that are fostered in an infant–toddler room. Each group will provide opportunities for the kinds of interactions and activities that they hope will reinforce desirable relationships and prevent undesirable ones. In this way, Duck (1999) reminds us that relationships take place as individuals conduct the rest of their lives – at the workplace, in the early years centre, in leisure activities, and so on. Membership in any context will provide opportunities for relatedness, simply because membership brings certain people together and keeps others apart.

Other individual factors

Individual characteristics such as temperaments, capabilities and time in the lifespan all contribute towards the characteristics of any particular relationship. The kind of relationship, for example, sought by those who are shy will differ from those of non-shy individuals, as will the means used to initiate those relationships in the first place. The process of relating to others will also be shaped by the social, emotional and cognitive capabilities and skills of the individuals involved. Finally, the age of the individual will contribute to the kinds of relationships that are formed and maintained. Not only do individuals develop new skills and capabilities with age, but also they will be influenced by their own and their communities' expectations about the kinds of relationship that are appropriate at that stage in their lives (Duck, 1999; Takahashi, 2005; Degotardi *et al.*, 2013).

Relationship functions

So far, we have seen how relationships are tied to social and cultural worlds in which individual and group beliefs, expectations and needs intersect with interactions past, present and future. In Chapter 1 we explained how children are born into, and progressively enter, many social contexts, including those of their families, social and cultural groups, early childhood services, schools and other institutions. Each context comprises a network of different relationships, and as individuals move between social contexts, these relationships interconnect with and influence one another. The result is that different relationships will have similarities as the interaction patterns and expectations of one context are transferred to that of another. However, as each relationship is located within a specific social environment, with its own expectations, systems of beliefs and practices, each relationship can also be expected to have dimensional qualities that differentiate it from other relationships in the child's network.

The functional approach to human relationships allows us to explore these variations in terms of *why relationships matter*. The immediate issue at hand is not so much why relationships are important for future or long-term development and learning (as discussed in Chapter 1), but more so the function that any particular relationship serves in the lives of particular people, in a particular context and time. Brecht (1997) reflects this approach when he states that 'we go into or develop relationships with other people to fulfill particular needs that we have', and thus defines a relationship as 'the coming together of two or more people for their *mutual benefit*' (p. 2, italics added). By focusing on relationship functions, we are able to examine the meaning that any particular relationship holds for the individuals involved, as well as develop an understanding of why different relationships have different qualities and characteristics. This approach also draws attention to both psychological and behavioural aspects of relationships. Relationship functions are reflected in, and realized through, the particular dimensions and qualities of interpersonal interactions. The psychological aspect comprises the function that it serves, whether that be emotional, motivational, social or cognitive. These functions, though, cannot be considered without exploring behavioural aspects, in particular the unique characteristics of the interactions that take place between the relationship partners. As an example, the emotions that one might express, and behaviours that one might exhibit, are likely to differ considerably depending on the particular relationship within which they occur.

What are these different relationship functions, and what do they 'look like' in practice? In the next section, we address these questions, and begin to explore the various functions that can be satisfied by the relationships that occur in infant and toddler early childhood programmes. Our aim here is not to provide a comprehensive list of all the functions that can be achieved, but instead to illustrate the characteristics of different kinds of relationship, and illustrate how they were experienced by the children, educators and parents.

Research in focus: relationships perspectives

The evidence that forms the basis of this analysis was derived from data generated in the '*Relationships perspectives*' toddler-room case study. This study used observational methods to investigate the different types of relationship that were experienced by a class of 18- to 30-month-old children in an Australian long-day-care centre. The children were observed during their everyday experiences for a period of six weeks, during which the researcher (SD) photographed and wrote anecdotal observations of the children's interactions with educators and peers. Immediately after each observation day, the photographs and written notes were consulted, and narratives, combining the written description of the interaction and relevant photographs, were created to illustrate interactions which were judged by the researcher to typify different relationship dimensions and functions. These narratives were then shared with the room educators and the children's parents, who were asked to provide their ideas and viewpoints about the meaning and significance of the captured interactions.

In this chapter, we introduce 28-month-old Robert and 18-month-old Harry, who have both attended the centre on the same days for more than a year. In the following episode, which is developed across the course of the chapter, we see how the first 30 minutes of Robert's day plays out, observing his interactions with his mother, his teacher, Cathy, and peer, Harry.

Care, security and trust

It is first thing in the morning. Harry has already arrived and is playing contentedly in the outside sandpit with some push-along trucks. Robert arrives with his mother, who walks with him to the outside veranda. Robert appears to be walking reluctantly, pressing against his mother's legs as she moves outside. The teacher, Cathy, sees them and moves over to say hello. She crouches down and encourages Robert over to her – holding out her arms and saying 'Come and give me a hello hug, Robert.' Robert looks up, grins, and moves rapidly into Cathy's arms and they both hug boisterously and laugh. Robert's mum smiles as she watches the embrace, and she and Cathy then chat briefly about Robert's morning before she says goodbye. She gives Robert a kiss, and leaves. Robert remains in Cathy's arms and they both watch mum leave. He stays there a minute longer before starting to scan the playground.

One of the predominant functions of infant and toddler relationships with adults, whether they are parents or educator, is the provision of physical and emotional care. The recent focus on the applicability of attachment theory to early childhood contexts has drawn attention to how child–educator relationships contribute towards children's emotional security through the provision of protection, nurturance and care (Rolfe, 2004). Relationships that meet this function are characterized by emotionally warm and sensitive interactions, and it is through these interactions that adults demonstrate to children that they are available to to meet their emotional and physical needs (Butterfield, Martin and Prairie, 2004). In the observation above, we see examples of this availability, with Robert and his mother remaining close to one another as they enter the centre and Cathy moving quickly to provide physical reassurance. By being present, Cathy indicates to Robert that she is there for him, and that he can come to her for comfort and assistance when this is needed.

Responsiveness is a further dimension of this function, in which adults not only respond to young children's perceived feelings and needs ('How does this child feel?' and 'What does he need?'), but also consider their intentions ('What does he want?'). Cathy's actions – her prompt availability and her invitation to hug – and Robert's exhuberant response suggest that Cathy successfully tapped in to Robert's needs as well as his intentions. Trust is built between the child and adult, as consistent respectful and responsive interactions ensure that young children receive the emotional and physical care they need in order to feel safe and secure (Raikes, Edwards and Gandini, 2009). Both 'parties' in this relationship are clear about their needs and how these are being met in this relationship.

The establishment of trust is also widely regarded as an important quality of parent–educator relationships, and provides an emotional context in which parents and educators can gain a sense of confidence that the wellbeing and learning requirements of the child will be met (Brooker, 2010). Confidence is established over time, and opportunities to chat and share information assist parents and educators to feel comfortable with one another and in their shared commitment to the child. For both parent and educator, warmth, openness and sensitivity are seen as important foundations from which mutual trust and respect can be built (Keyes, 2002). Educators, in particular, value parents' willingness to share information about the child, as this allows them to develop confidence in their own ability to work with the child. Robert's mother's experience of the warm hug between Robert and Cathy may also contribute as parents have been reported to gain confidence and trust in their children's caregivers when they perceive that there is mutual affection and caring between that caregiver and their child (Elicker *et al.*, 1997).

Self-affirmation

Relationships also provide a sense of validation and self-affirmation. On one level, this function is satisfied simply by being acknowledged and respected by significant others, as evidenced in the interaction between Cathy, Robert and Robert's mother above. Furthermore, when children's perspectives are validated by educators who actively consider their intentions and opinions, their participatory rights are upheld and respected (Degotardi, 2013). The flip side of this is that self-affirmation also comes from being able to freely express and assert one's own wishes, needs and ideas to others. In a continuation of the observation documented above, it is evident that this function can feature in young children's relationships with their peers.

> Five minutes later, Robert has moved down to the sandpit area where Harry is still playing with the trucks. Robert also collects a truck and sits about a metre away from Harry, silently pushing a truck back and forth. Harry also pushes his truck, looks up at Robert and calls out 'Let's go Robert. Let's go.' Robert does not respond, so Harry repeats his invitation. Robert, however, holds tightly to his truck and says 'No.' Harry pushes his truck out of the sandpit and begins to climb up some steps towards the veranda. Robert watches him go, and then, still

holding on to his truck, begins to follow. Harry is struggling to move his truck up the steps, and Robert is soon alongside him and they ascend the steps together. Once on the veranda, Robert moves towards Cathy, who is standing next to a painting easel. Harry crawls past them, still pushing his truck, but Robert remains with Cathy and they are soon chatting quietly about how to attach the paper to the easel. Cathy explains to him how she needs the pegs to attach the paper, and asks Robert to retrieve two from the peg container. Robert complies, and holds the paper against the easel while Cathy attaches the pegs.

In this interaction, Harry and Robert both express and assert their individual wants and thoughts. Harry reaches out, issuing an invitation to play and thus communicates his intentions to Robert. Robert asserts himself by refusing, and Harry accepts his choice and continues in his play. During such exchanges, children are presented with opportunities to compare themselves to others, thus contributing towards a sense of self-in-relation-to-others (Mead, 1934). Self-affirmation also comes in the form of the negotiation of power and control, which is a frequent theme in studies of interpersonal relationships (Noller *et al.*, 2001). Despite their initial incompatible goals, Harry and Robert appear comfortable enough in their relationship with each other (and others around them) to pursue their own interests and thus maintain an element of control over their individual play.

Companionship, collaboration and social participation

While the extract above illustrates elements of individuality, it also demonstrates how relationships function to provide company and affiliation. Robert chooses to sit close to Harry and selects a similar toy to play with in an apparent move towards togetherness, which characterizes early friendships (Avgitidou, 2001). Although there is an initial refusal to play together, Robert is seemingly drawn towards Harry's company when he follows him up the steps, and thus demonstrates a preference to be with him and join his activity rather than to continue to play alone. Peer relationships are a rich source of companionship, providing playmates and conversational partners who share interests and collectively pursue goals (Rose-Krasnor and Denham, 2009). Yet in early childhood, companionship can also be provided by adults, as evidenced by the interaction between Robert and Cathy, and such interactions provide opportunities for learning and teaching. Cathy appears to respond to Robert's interest by talking to him about the mechanics of attaching the paper to the easel, and capitalizes on their relationships to provide a valuable learning opportunity. She continues to permit his active participation as they cooperate to achieve a shared goal, and therefore not only provides opportunities for Robert to acquire new skills and knowledge, but also to gain experience in socially accepted ways of participating. A further example is provided below:

Robert has now rejoined Harry in the sandpit. He points to the sandpit edge and says 'Harry – there's lots of sand there – Harry,' but Harry is engrossed in his truck play and appears not to respond. A moment later, though, Harry begins to say 'Beep, beep', looks up at Robert and repeats 'Robert – beep, beep!' The two boys now push their trucks back and forth, occasionally making 'beep, beep' sounds in unison. Robert notices a broom nearby and goes to collect it. Putting it next to Harry, he says 'Harry – here's your broom.' Robert then goes to Cathy to ask for a broom. He returns carrying his newly acquired broom and Harry, noticing, asks 'Robert – where's my broom?' Robert looks round and points to the one that he had brought across earlier. The two boys then begin sweeping the edge of the sandpit together. A conversation develops between the two boys that revolves largely around their possessions. Robert picks up a truck and says 'I've got a truck', to which Harry replies 'Where's my truck?', and then immediately finds one and plays with this too. This initiation and response went both ways:

Harry: 'I've got a brush.'

Robert: 'Where's my brush?'

Robert: 'Harry, I found a stick.'

Harry: 'Where's my stick?'

Harry: 'Robert, I've got a digger.'

Robert: 'I've got a digger too.'

Relationships provide children with opportunities to become socialized into the broader expectations and accepted practices of the group (Noller *et al.*, 2001). In the extract above, peer group expectations come into play, as themes of 'ownership' and 'sharing' are negotiated during Robert and Harry's playful interactions. Such interactions allow participants to model and be exposed to acceptable behaviours within that particular context, as well as to gain immediate feedback about the acceptability of their own behaviour. As evidenced above, relationships also involve patterns of 'give and take', where similarities and differences are negotiated, where common ground is sought, and where individuality is balanced with the interests of others. By stressing joint participation, such interactions provide entry into group membership and, according to Noller *et al.* (2001), afford 'the lessons in the benefits that group belonging can provide' (p. 40).

Different relationships – different functions

One of the advantages of exploring relationships from a functional perspective is that it permits the examination of opportunities for learning, teaching and support that are inherent in the range of relationships that are formed between individuals. While each relationship in any person's relationships network will have its own set of dimensions, it is expected that any one relationship may satisfy many different functions (Brecht, 1997). Depending on a range of social, cultural and individual factors, these functions will be met to varying extents by different kinds of relationship.

This idea has particular relevance to early childhood education as it allows us to gain a deeper understanding of the opportunities for development and learning that each relationship may provide. Because infant–toddler rooms are inhabited with many different individuals who have varying roles, these different individuals are motivated to engage in different types of interactions and activities with the child. The result is that, by weaving in and out of a range of relationships, children will participate in a range of experiences, all of which will differ in interaction quality and style depending on the interests and priorities of those involved. Relationships can therefore be conceptualized from a pedagogical perspective – as contexts in which distinct forms of learning and development may be promoted or constrained, depending on the type of relationship, and the needs and priorities of those involved (Shpancer, 2002).

A different perspective: understanding relationships through parents' and educators' points of view

An advantage of the functional approach is that it focuses strongly on the real-world meaning that is attached to different relationships by all who are involved. As well as gaining insights into how relationships contribute to the quality of lives of those who directly experience the relationship, these daily lives extend beyond the immediate concerns of the individuals to incorporate the significance that other people in children's lives ascribe to their relationships (Duck, 1999). As major stakeholders in their children's lives and learning, the perspectives of educators and parents provide additional meaning to children's relationships by locating these relationships within children's broader social-experiential world. As explained in Chapter 2, the views and understandings of major stakeholders in early childhood programmes comprise an important aspect of evidence that early childhood services can consider when engaging in professional decision-making (Buysse and Wesley, 2006). By understanding educators' perspectives it is possible to gain an understanding of the motivations behind decisions about which kinds of relationships to foster and which kinds to discourage. Parents' perspectives provide a broader understanding of the family values and priorities that children bring with them into the centre, and of the concerns of parents as they seek to provide their children with early experiences that are consistent with their views. Explorations of parents' and educators' relationship perspectives therefore enhance understandings of the social-contextual foundation of the relationships that children form in their centres, as well as the role that these relationships can play in their lives (Degotardi et al., 2013).

In this final section, we examine the perspectives of parents and educators by revisiting the documented observation above. After reading the photo-narrative of this episode, Robert's mother raised the significance of security and trust when she discussed Robert's willingness to go to Cathy on arrival:

Initially there's that hesitancy of leaving me, but now in the morning when he sees Cathy – because he's close to Cathy now – there's that instant connection. And I go, 'Do you want to go to Cathy?' And he says, 'Yes, I want to go to Cathy', and he just opens up his arms and goes, 'I want to go to Cathy.'

In contrast, Cathy focused on Robert's initial hesitation, and attributed this to a possible break in routine as well as perceived different relationship dynamics between Robert, his mother and his father:

Dad's the usual drop off, and he's pretty much fine. You'll say, 'Come on let's go', and he'll come straight to me. Whereas if it's Mum, he does a bit of 'I don't want to go.'

When discussing the relationship between the two boys, Cathy drew attention to what she viewed as interesting power dynamics when she offered the following point of view:

It's quite interesting, because Robert tends to be the leader in the group and likes to have control over what they do. And it's quite interesting because Harry's fighting for that too . . . Robert's got a strong personality and he'll just do what he wants, I suppose. If he doesn't cooperate with Harry, like before, Harry would get upset. But he's [referring to Harry] got over that. So he just went off and did his own thing.

Cathy explained how the quality of the playful behaviours between the two boys was changing as these power dynamics were shifting. Harry, she stated, was starting to assert himself, while Robert, in Cathy's words, was '*cooperating a bit more*'.

Another educator, Hasumi, focused on the friendship between the two boys, expressing the opinion that it was partly due to opportunity, explaining that the closeness between the two boys was because '*they all come every day . . . because they see each other every day*'. She went on to focus on the importance of companionship, stating that Robert, Harry and another child, Ali, '*are very close. They are interested in the same things, like trucks and the construction things.*' The third educator, Min-Jee, was similar in her account, explaining that:

They always they look for each other and they like to do something together – play. They know if they play with the same things they can play close.

Harry's father also mentioned friendship and the social participation that this brought, stating that the boys were *as "thick as thieves". They seem to do everything together.'* In contrast to Hasumi, though, Harry's father also focused on self-assertion, stating:

I've noticed a couple of times when I get here in the afternoon and the three boys are still here, they'll be doing whatever they're doing and they'll have a truck or a digger by their side. And no one else can have it.

Harry's father explained that Harry often defended his possessions at home when he asserted his own wants and needs when playing with his sister. Similarly, Robert's mother placed both the power dynamics and the negotiation of possessions in the context of the family, explaining that Robert often had disputes over belongings with his older sister:

But they do have sort of conflicts as in Robert will say 'It's mine, it's mine' . . . I think he actually plays up to the fact that he is younger . . . he starts to cry. And I know it's not a real cry, it's more of an attempt at 'I want, so I should have.' But I know that with certain things, like with his toys and trucks, you have to ask permission. You have to say 'Robert, can Keira have a go?' and then he understands that and goes 'Okay.'

The expectations around the possession of the trucks therefore became the topic of discussion about how the relationship reflected and reinforced the boys' understanding of social expectations. In the centre context Min-Jee explained that *'they have a rule. If there's someone playing first, they both wait.'* In this way, educators and parents positioned the observed behaviours within the context of the social expectations of the family and the peer group, and acknowledged how the dynamics of different relationships in these children's social network will impact on those formed in the centre.

Whose perspective matters?

It is interesting to note how parents and educators brought a range of perspectives to the same episode. They all demonstrated concern with understanding the unique nature of interactions between children, children and parents, children and educators, as well as parents and educators. However, not only did they notice and choose to discuss different aspects of the narrative, but, collectively, their perspectives demonstrate how the same interaction behaviours can be interpreted according to a range of different ideas. While, at first glance, these varied perspectives could seem contradictory, in actuality they add contextual richness to these children's relationship experiences. Taken together, these snapshots of relationship dynamics and functions support contemporary notions of early childhood relationships as reflecting a complex web of belief systems, perspectives and pragmatic needs. They provide an insight into the many individual, social and cultural forces that interact to bring about the particular relationship dynamics between these two boys, their educators and parents (Duck, 1999). By taking note of the multiple interpretations, we can see how the relationship experiences that occurred in a very short period of time in the centre are interwoven with those that occur at home and how histories of past experiences have combined to give rise to current patterns of interaction. Instead of being points of difference, the perspectives of educators and parents thus combine to provide a deeper and socially meaningful account of the relationships that occur in the centre.

Some final thoughts

Viewed in the context of these varying perspectives and needs, the 'sites of struggle' referred to in Chapter 2 are not surprising. Early childhood educators today must contend with and embrace an array of influences and points of view, some of which are likely to contrast, if not conflict, with their own deeply held values and beliefs. In establishing positive relationships with children and their caregivers, early childhood educators need to be encouraged to create space for themselves and important others within the early childhood settings to establish mutual care and trust on the basis of open understanding of one another's priorities and customs.

Contemporary perspectives on relationships, therefore, tend to reflect Moore's (2007) argument that effective relationships require consideration and effort:

> The starting point for all effective relationships is tuning to the other person's world, understanding their perspective and experience, and establishing a personal connection.

(p. 5)

Chapter 4, which focuses on the formation of new relationships during the transition into formal care settings, further highlights this emerging contention that, rather than being predetermined by sets of instructions or formulae that guarantee success, effective relationships in early childhood settings are grounded in mutual respect and care, benefited significantly by each party's willingness to engage in a process of getting to know each other, sharing ideas and 'establishing' a personal connection.

4 Forming relationships: transitioning into the group setting

You can't stay in your corner of the forest waiting for others to come to you. You have to go to them sometimes.

A.A. Milne (1926)

A reality of human existence is that we all, at various points in our lives, move out of our 'corner of the forest' to encounter new people, situations and settings. When we enter into these new contexts, we experience a period of transition during which we become familiar with, and adapt to, the new environment. Transitions are periods of adjustment and change in which people react and respond to novel experiences. They are times when individuals develop knowledge about, and become comfortable in, their new, unfamiliar situation. Even when transitions are straightforward, they involve growth and development, as individuals develop new strategies and understandings that will enable them to function emotionally, socially, physically and cognitively in their new setting (Lee, 2006; Jung, 2011). In terms of a relationships focus, transitions represent periods of learning in which individuals' capacity to learn how to relate to new people and events can shape the extent to which transitions are largely positive or negative experiences (Cryer *et al.*, 2005).

Entrance into an early childhood centre can signify one of the first major transitions in a young child's life (Datler *et al.*, 2012). Not only do infants and toddlers have to adjust to the physical and social features of their new setting, but they also have to come to terms with separation from their parent or previous caregiver, and get to know new caregivers. It is therefore little wonder that transition into early childhood settings is an unsettling experience, often associated with distress, feelings of insecurity and social inhibitions (Ahnert *et al.*, 2004; Datler *et al.*, 2012).

In this chapter, we will explore different processes that are associated with the transitions that occur as a young child enters the early childhood centre. We begin by addressing the challenge of the transition period for infants, educators and families, before then characterizing this period as one of relationship formation and realignment. We then use data from the *Making Connections: The Dynamics of Relationship Formation* study to discuss different ways of understanding relationship formation in three areas: educator–infant relationships, educator–parent relationships and infant–peer relationships.

The challenge of transitions

While the transition to the early childhood centre can be challenging for all involved, research demonstrates that unsettled behaviour and feelings of distress generally decrease with time. Children who have spent more time in early childhood centres tend to be more content, more involved with peers and less reliant on their adult caregivers than those with less experience (National Institute of Child Health and Human Development Early Child Care Research Network, 2001; Deynoot-Schaub and Risken-Walraven, 2006; Datler *et al.*, 2012). Nevertheless, the settling-in process *does* take time, especially with the youngest children, for whom a number of months can pass before they feel comfortable in their new setting (Fein, Gariboldi and Raffaella, 1993; Cryer *et al.*, 2005).

The transition is not only challenging for infants and toddlers, but also for educators and parents. These adults are very aware of the stress that infants and toddlers can experience when they first start childcare, and often draw on their own emotional and social resilience to support young children's adjustment (Gonzalez-Mena and Widmeyer Eyer, 2007). Parents, in particular, can experience a range of emotions when their young children make the early transition from home to formalized care. During the transition phase, parents and educators are also getting to know and feel comfortable with one another, and the quality of their early interactions will have a direct bearing on the infant or toddler's experience at the centre. Frequent and open parent–educator communication builds up the educators' knowledge of, and empathy with, individual child needs, interests and learning styles (Brooker, 2009). Also, friendly and supportive interactions can reduce stress levels in both infants and adults (Jovanovic, 2011).

Transition to childcare centres as a period of relationship formation

Brooker (2009) describes transitions as a period of settling in, of establishing familiarity and reducing the negative impact of a novel situation. From this perspective, newcomers are integrated into the setting, gaining a sense of belonging and of 'feeling suitable' within their new environment. Brooker explains that transitions represent key periods of relationship formation where each individual gradually comes to know others in the centre. It is a period where the many relationships experienced by infants and toddlers intersect, where family relationship dynamics meet centre relationship dynamics, and where the relationship characteristics, opportunities and expectations of one community influence and interact with one another. In short, it is a time when these young children's relationship worlds will expand and change considerably.

Hinde (1997) links transition processes to relationship formation by describing this period as 'a process of uncertainty reduction – uncertainty about that individual as a potential partner and uncertainty about the relationship' (p. 461). Uncertainty is experienced in the here-and-now, as individuals negotiate the boundaries and expectations related to the kinds of interactions and behaviours occurring within that relationship. Uncertainty is also linked to previous relationship history, as the relationship characteristics that individuals have experienced in the past need to be reconciled with the characteristics of the newly forming relationships. Finally, there is uncertainty about the future – not only of whether a relationship will endure the test of time, but also whether it will have the desired benefits, or outcomes, for the people involved. Overcoming this uncertainty represents a key step not only in making positive transitions but also in forming positive relationships.

While each individual brings past experiences and future projections to any new relationship, a genuine relationship is formed by both partners' engagement in dynamic and dyadic processes of negotiation and change. Changes occur at the personal level, as the individual begins to view him or herself in the context of the new relationship, and at the relationship level, as the joint contributions of each individual define the nature of the forming relationship (Duck, 1999). In this regard, Hinde (1997) explains that the 'Growth of a relationship depends in large measure on what the partners do together' (p. 463) and thus stresses the point that interactions play a vital role in this process. In the early stages of a relationship, interactions enable an individual to discern the intentions, feelings and actions of the other towards the self, allowing feelings of trust and comfort between the two individuals. Repeated interactions provide opportunities for views to be exchanged and negotiated, resulting in the discovery and establishment of shared interests, values and practices which, as explained in Chapter 3, ultimately characterize the quality and type of the relationship that will be formed.

Research in focus: *Making Connections: The Dynamics of Relationship Formation*

In this chapter, we use observational and interview data from the *Making Connections* project to explore some processes involved in three infants' transition into an infant–toddler room. This research was carried out over a period of three months, and documented the experiences of three infants and their families as they transitioned into an infant–toddler room in Sydney, Australia. During this period, we took extensive video-recorded observations of these infants and their experiences with educators and peers. We also spoke regularly with their families and early childhood teacher, Tabitha, to determine what they felt were important factors relating to how these young children formed relationships as they transitioned into the infant-toddler-room.

Here, we focus on the experiences of these three toddlers and their families as they transitioned into the childcare centre: 15-month-old Ben was the second child of Jerome and Clare and younger sibling of Aiden, who attended the preschool room. Bella had just turned 1 when she started at the centre. The third child of Linda and David, Bella's 7-year-old sister, attended the centre before her and her 4-year-old brother currently attended the preschool room. Matthew, at 8 months, was the youngest child in the room. The first child of Rebecca and Andrew, and first grandchild on both sides of the family, Matthew had spent the first months of his life being cared for at home by his parents and grandparents, and his parents warmly described him as being the 'centre of attention'.

Early days

Since transition to the early childhood centre involves separation of the young child from their parent, it is not surprising that most early childhood texts include sections on how to address the anxiety that accompanies this period. Advice is provided to educators to put systems in place to increase the likelihood that parents will, for example, avoid making 'a quick escape' or staying too long, remain confident and positive, and establish a predictable transition routine (Wittmer and Petersen, 2009). Such advice is supported by research. For example, in an observational study of the separation behaviours of 24 Israeli infant–parent dyads, Klein, Kraft and Shohet (2010) described a typical *separation ceremony*, or predictable sequence of events, including the child being carried in to the room, greetings and information exchange between caregiver, parent and child, the storing of belongings and the setting of the child at an activity in the room. Parents then indicated to the caregiver their intent to leave, and the caregiver stepped in to replace the parent or wave goodbye with the child.

These researchers argue that the predictability of a separation ceremony helps both child and parent to develop strategies to cope with the distress of separation. Their findings provide valuable strategies to educators who seek to ease transition stress for all involved. However, while Klein and colleagues acknowledge that the transition process is a 'delicate yet complex interplay between parent, child and caregiver variables' (p. 388), they portray the transition period as primarily a period of learning by the parent, who needs to learn to 'understand and adjust to their infant's needs' (p. 394) in order to minimize the stress experienced by their child.

A different perspective: *Inserimento*

In contrast with the focus on managing separation, other approaches focus more strongly on the transition period as a time of relationship and community building. One such approach has been established in the infant–toddler centres in Reggio Emilia, Italy, where the concept of *Inserimento* describes intentional strategies used to help young children and their families settle in to the new environment (Bove, 2001). This settling-in period is recognized as a time of beginning relationships, with a focus on 'delicately' supporting the child and the family as they adjust to a new community in the infant–toddler room. It begins well before the first day of enrolment, with parents and children invited in to the centre to spend extended periods of time getting to know one another, the centre, and the staff and other children before they leave their child for the first time. While the ultimate aim is to enable the individual child to feel secure and comfortable in their new context, the transition period is focused on building new relationships with multiple others within the group.

Taking time

Many centres have drawn from *Inserimento* principles to foster relationship-building in the first few months of attendance. It is understood that the process takes time, as familiarity and security is built up gradually as parents, children and educators spend time together. One key feature of *Inserimento* that distinguishes it from the type of approach outlined earlier in this section is that, instead of focusing on separation issues, it is concerned with supporting closeness and intimacy between parent and child, as it is this closeness that supports the child's increasing confidence in their new environment. Some of the discussions that we had with teachers and parents fit with this notion. A few weeks after Ben commenced at his new centre, Ben's teacher, Tabitha, described how closeness played out during his earliest visits with his mother:

Ben came and visited last year a number of times, which was really nice that he and Clare came in . . . So when Ben started, he didn't want to leave mum's side, really, or if he did it was for a short time. And he continued to be clingy for most of that first week. But then his time away from mum would get longer and longer . . . When mum's here now, he doesn't have to be with mum. And he used to cling on to mum's skirt, and he doesn't have to do that now. So he's got that confidence about being here.

Confidence is also gained by parents as they are welcomed into the centre to experience the normal daily events in the classroom and allay any concerns that they may have about how their own child will adjust to the new context. When describing Matthew's earliest days, for example, Tabitha recalled;

Mum was a bit apprehensive that he may not eat our food, so she brought her food instead and continued to do that for the first week. But she's over that now! It was like 'He's eating, so that's fine.'

Educators also benefit from the extended opportunities to converse informally with parents, and to observe and interact with the child in the presence of the parent (Jovanovic, 2011). All of this contributes to a gradual process of getting to know the child and parent in the context of both family and centre life. Instead of being a time of stress and anxiety, the transition phase can be seen as 'a time when all involved value the pleasure of getting to know one another closely' (Bove, 2001, p. 114).

Constructing a network of relationships

One further important aspect of *Inserimento* is that it recognizes the network of relationships that exist and impact on one another within the group infant–toddler setting. Children benefit from seeing friendly and supportive inter-actions between parents and educators, and, as parents also begin to get comfortable with others in the room, this can work to gradually ease the child into a community that includes multiple adults and children. Tabitha showed her appreciation for Matthew's mother's engagement with all of the other children in the room as follows:

When she's [Rebecca] in the room, she does definitely engage with all the children in the room, and not just Matthew, which is one of the things that we love . . . So she is definitely paying everyone in the room attention, not just Matthew – showing him that there are other people in the room that matter. And so she's building up those relationships so hopefully then he will build up the relationships.

This excerpt from discussions with Matthew's teacher also captures Rebecca's own concern with facilitating positive relationship experiences for her son. In our discussions with her she eloquently explained, through reference to her own experiences as a child, why this was so important for her as a mother:

I guess I was always afraid of things. So if it was something new, like if we had to start a new course in music, or sport or something like that, I'd always be anxious the night before. I don't know why – just that anxious feeling of something that was changing – like routine was changing. So I guess I just want him to be happy and confident . . . My sister, who's 18 months younger than me, she said to Mum, across four lanes of traffic [on her first day of school – *author*], 'I'll be alright from here, Mum.' She didn't let Mum take her to the front gate. And Mum didn't know what was more heart-breaking – taking me when I cried every morning, or my sister that just said, 'I'll be alright from here, Mum.' We're very different.

Our data fit neatly with the principles of *Inserimento*, which in emphasizing the length of time taken to build relationships, acknowledges that relationships between parents, children and educators in childcare settings will be unique in nature, both across settings and for each individual relationship (Brooker, 2010). Each parent/family enters in to the childcare centre with a unique set of experiences and expectations that impact in important ways on the transition experiences and behaviours, particularly of very young children. During our observations, we noted the strong preference for close physical contact by particular children. Our conversations with Linda, whose daughter, Bella, enjoyed constant 'cuddles' with her teacher, illustrated for us the influence of home experiences and relationships on the development of new relationships in the centre. Also, importantly, the need for preferences based on experience at home to be supported in the formation of relationships developed in the childcare centre:

Early on – and she doesn't do it so much with me any more – but she was still doing it . . . when she's particularly tired and wants a really big cuddle she'll tuck her hands right into your bra. And Tabitha said to Andrew [father], 'Is she still being breastfed?' And Andrew's like, 'No.' And I was wondering . . . There's just that nice little pocket there. And I was really interested that she was doing it as well with whoever she obviously needed the security from at [childcare centre]. So I thought that was nice that she's obviously not too shy . . .

Sue [teacher] was telling me on Friday morning that she was giving lovely kisses to them all in the preschool room at some stage. So I don't know when that was, but she was obviously . . . So she must be starting to feel at home generally all around. Which is good.

The intimate and complex nature of relationships (and how they are built) expressed so beautifully here fits with a theoretical approach to understanding contexts of parenting and behaviour described by cultural psychologists who are interested in understanding how parenting is infused by social and cultural beliefs or practices. Shweder, Goodnow, Hatano, Levine, Markus and Miller (1998) have referred to the inherent links between what people feel and believe and what they do as an 'intimate association between a mentality and a practice' (p. 872). Perhaps the most useful insight offered by this concept, applied to the 'art' of understanding how relationships are built with parents and young children during periods of transition, is that the values, beliefs and expectations that underpin positive relationships formation can be so inherent that they are taken for granted. This means that, while understanding such values and beliefs is essential for forming relationships, it can be complex, because they are often not communicated openly in daily conversations and/or interactions." In building positive relationships, it is therefore important to focus not only on the concrete expectations of parents regarding interactions within early childhood settings, but also on the underlying influences that are likely to shape these expectations.

Once we've said goodbye: establishing educator–child relationships

As well as being a period of relationship formation, the transition to the early childhood centre involves relationship realignment as the young child's relationship world gradually changes to incorporate the other adults and children in the room (Wittmer and Petersen, 2009). Children and educators are learning about one another and, as new children gradually become used to events and people within the new environment without the presence of their parents, new relationships are formed (Dalli, 2000). Once parents have left, attention is often paid to the processes of establishing and building a deep and secure relationship between the educators and the new children on the basis that this relationship provides a foundation for children's adjustment, learning and subsequent relationships (Lee, 2006). In this next section, we focus on Ben's early experiences in the centre in order to illustrate some of the ways that this adjustment was experienced by Ben and the infant room staff.

I'm still here

Physical closeness and availability are often identified by both parents and educators as significant means of comforting young children, and establishing a sense of security and trust (Ebbeck and Yim, 2008). Dalli (2000), reporting on her observational case study of toddler Sarah's transitional experiences, describes how Sarah's teacher provided a constant presence in the absence of her mother. Being always by her side, the teacher could physically hold and comfort Sarah when she was upset, and provide Sarah with the security of knowing that she was there to help and support her while her mother was not there. In some centres, it is the practice that a primary caregiver is allocated to each new infant, on the basis that relationship adjustment is supported when these emotional and care needs can be met in a consistent manner by one other person (Rockel, 2005). In Ben's case, the centre did not have this policy but instead responded to its observations of each child to determine who that child was naturally gravitating towards. Tabitha explained that she found that most children *'naturally seem to choose someone – they find who they want to be with and we let them do that'*. In Ben's case, Tabitha identified educator Kellie as that person, and explained this preference in terms of Kellie's availability to provide physical comfort at the significant time of separation:

I think Kellie is that person for him . . . it's been a few times that Kellie has been there for the drop-off, and so has said goodbye to mum and dad with Ben, so she has been there for that tender time. She has comforted for that time and that's lingered on for the day.

In contrast to Dalli's detailed description of Sarah and her teacher, Ben did not appear to need or want a constant close physical presence with Kellie, and was often observed to be watching other children some distance from her, or playing quietly by himself. However, as the following observation illustrates, Kellie's presence still provided reassurance, and Kellie responded to this need by communicating her willingness to be available should he need her:

Ben has been standing outside watching the activity of his peers. Kellie walks by, looks down at Ben, and smiles. He remains expressionless but establishes and maintains eye contact with Kellie. Kellie stops and asks 'Where would you like to go?' Ben does not respond but holds his gaze. Kellie points to the sandpit: 'This way?' and then gestures towards inside, 'Or will we go this way?' Kellie begins to move into the room and Ben pauses before following her inside. Kellie turns and waits, allowing him to join her. A while later, Ben and Kellie are sitting together playing with some cardboard tubes. Kellie moves briefly away from the area in order to assist another child. Ben immediately moves as if to follow her. Kellie notices, turns and smiles, saying 'I'm still here' and Ben remains, but watches Kellie until she returns.

Transitional objects

The presence of a familiar adult is not the only means of 'filling the gap' left by the separation process. Winnicott introduced the concept of the *transitional object* to refer to an object or event that is used by the child to provide a sense of security and to establish a way of remaining connected to an absent parent (Page *et al.*, 2013). In Ben's case, an important classroom fixture emerged:

It is a short time after Ben's father has left the centre, and Ben is standing by a large photo frame attached to the wall which contains photographs of many of the children and their families. Kellie walks past and Ben moves after her, calling 'Papa, papa.' Kellie turns: 'Can you show me?' Ben walks to the frame and points to the photograph of his family, and repeats 'Papa.' Kellie says 'Yes – Papa is at work', and Ben then points to and names 'mama' and his brother, Aiden. Kellie confirms that 'Mama is at work' and 'Aiden is in the preschool room.'

According to Winnicott, the importance of a transitional object lies in how it is used by the child to represent the relationship between the child and the missing parent (Davar, 2001). The transitional object is therefore a bridging object that eases the transition between home and centre-based relationships. Ben's teacher Tabitha explained '*there will be a time when he does get upset and he will go to the picture again*' thus suggesting that, through this ritual, Ben was able to re-establish the feeling of security that the relationship with his family provided.

The significance of the object is not the object itself, but what that object represents for the child. With time, the reliance on the object, like the reliance on the presence of the parent, may diminish. However, as illustrated below, the familiar, ritualized connection between home and family can appear in other contexts:

It is a couple of weeks later, and Ben is outside. He approaches Tabitha, pointing outside of the fence and saying 'Papa, papa.' Tabitha responds with the now familiar 'Papa is at work.' Ben smiles and holds out both hands, repeating 'Papa.' Tabitha holds his hands and sways them while she chants 'Papa is at work. Mama is at work. Aiden is in the preschool room – Hurrah! And Ben is in the nur-ser-y – Hooray!' Ben smiles and repeats 'Papa', which Tabitha interprets as an invitation to repeat the chant.

While acknowledging Ben's need for reassurance, Tabitha suggests that, with time, the nature of the ritual had changed:

It used to be comfort, but now it's turned into play. Because he's happy to play, and doesn't need that comfort any more.

Tabitha's comment highlights how relationships gradually change in dynamics and functions across the transition period. The transitional object, it appeared, had served its purpose, and the increasingly confident and comfortable Ben was now prepared to move towards a more playful relationship with the educators in the room.

Rethinking sensitivity

When considering how infants and toddlers form relationships with their caregivers, it is impossible to overlook the crucial role of sensitive caregiving. This emphasis is supported by an extensive body of research that identifies sensitivity as an important factor in attachment security, both at home and in early childhood settings (Ahnert, Pinquart and Lamb, 2006). One of the first researchers to identify the significance of sensitivity was Mary Ainsworth (Ainsworth, Bell and Stayton, 1974; Ainsworth, 1979), who investigated which maternal interaction behaviours were related to secure and insecure attachments between mothers and their infants. Sensitivity, she explained, is an observable, behavioural trait, comprising a number of behaviours that demonstrate attunement, and responsiveness to the child's activity, emotions and intentions. Since that time, sensitivity has become known as a broad and multidimensional concept that includes:

- *emotional* sensitivity, including responding appropriately to the infant's emotional states as well as being emotionally available and expressive to the infant
- *physical* sensitivity, including responding promptly to physical needs such as hunger, tiredness and pain
- *behavioural* sensitivity, including responding to infants' bids for attention, supporting their movements and explorations, imitating and responding to vocalizations, and sustaining joint activities
- *cognitive* sensitivity, including appropriate pacing, scaffolding, encouragement and interventions (Tamis-LeMonda, 1996).

What underpins all of these behaviours is the caregiver's ability to consider the young child's perspective – to notice their cues and interpret what those cues mean in terms of how the child is feeling, what they are trying to do, and how they are understanding the experience (Meins *et al.*, 2001; Degotardi and Sweller, 2012). Sensitivity therefore comprises more than an ability to respond to infant behaviours, but also a level of perceptiveness to the individual contributions of the child who brings their own ideas and intentions to any relationship-building interaction. This idea moves away from viewing sensitivity solely as an aspect of the caregiver's behaviour to thinking about it as a characteristic of the interaction that involves contributions of both caregiver and infant. This point of view is proposed by Lee (2006), who argues that 'both infant and caregiver need time and opportunities to understand each other's behaviour and cues and to adjust themselves to each other' (p. 134).

From this perspective, reciprocity is stressed, as the infant and the educator respond to each other and get to know each other's signals, as well as their personality, interaction and learning styles. Lee (2006) stresses that the establishment of such interactions takes time, and is contingent on the gradual establishment of a level of trust and security beforehand. This was certainly the case with Ben, with his early interactions with educators focusing on an emotional need for security and home-connection. Once this need was fulfilled, he could relax into the kind of mutually playful and expressive interactions that Lee characterizes as the final stage of relationship formation:

Ben is playing at a low table with some containers and small toy animals. Hayley approaches and sits next to him. She picks up a toy and puts it in a container. Ben looks up and grins at her and then puts a block into the same container. Hayley watches and chats with him about what he is doing: 'There goes another one. And another!' Ben looks up and grins after he puts each one in. He places the lid on the container, then, picking the lid up swiftly, he says 'Boo!' Hayley laughs and says 'Oh – Boo!' in return. Ben replaces the lid on to the container, and Hayley holds her hands out in an inquiring gesture, asking 'Where's he gone?' Ben smiles, removes the lid again, and repeats 'Boo!' at which both he and Hayley laugh.

In this final stage, Lee (2006) describes the contribution of educator and infant as being 'highly in step in their play/interactions, they become interactive, sometimes leading and sometimes following' (p. 139). Through this process of give and take, infant and educators become full partners in the kind of synchronous, *mutually sensitive* interactions from which a positive and developmentally supportive educator–child relationship can grow.

Fostering peer relationships

While educator–child relationship formation is undoubtedly an essential feature aspect of any young child's relationship network, group-care contexts provide unique opportunities for children to develop relationships with their peers. In the past, many considered that infants' and toddlers' capacity to relate to others was reflected predominantly with adults. More recent research has challenged this assumption, demonstrating that even very young children have the capacity and motivation to engage socially with peers (Hay, Payne and Chadwick, 2004). In this next section, we explore some of the ways in which peer relationships are formed as infants and toddlers transition into a group-care setting.

It has long been recognized that the ways in which young children form relationships with their peers depend, in part, on the quality of the relationships they have with significant others. The recent focus on attachment theory within early childhood contexts has seen the accumulation of research evidence to suggest that infants' early attachments with significant adults have implications for their ability to form positive peer relationships. Longitudinal data, for example, has demonstrated that secure mother–infant attachment is related to less peer-related aggression at age 3, and more positive friendship interactions at age 5 (McElwain *et al.*, 2003; McElwain, Booth-Laforce and Wu, 2011). Within the childcare centre, the quality of the attachment relationship between young children and their educators or caregivers has also been found to be linked to peer social competence, with securely attached children demonstrating higher levels of social-interactive play behaviours and lower levels of aggression than their insecurely attached peers (e.g. Howes, Hamilton and Hamilton, 1994; Howes, Hamilton and Philipsen, 1998). Such studies suggest that the relationship representation constructed by young children during their interactions with adults serves to inform the nature of subsequent relationships with peers. Certainly, the observation that the majority of infants' initial interactions on entering childcare rooms tend to be with adults, highlights the significance of the adult–infant relationships as a foundation for relationships with others (Datler *et al.*, 2012).

A different perspective: the importance of intentional teaching

Although findings such as those described above are persuasive as to the significance of the adult–infant attachment, they do little to inform us about the actual processes that are involved with infants' and toddlers' relationship formation with their peers. Questions remain about the strategies that infant–toddler educators use to foster relationship formation between these very young peers. Pedagogical approaches to peer relationships draw attention to how educators provide structure and guidance to maximize the opportunities that young children have to interact and form relationships with one another. Writing about infant and toddler peer relationships, Wittmer (2008) makes the claim that 'Children learn about themselves and others *with* the significant adults in their lives' (p. 24, italics added). If this is the case, then there is a need to consider which teaching strategies can be used to intentionally support peer relationship formation within the early childhood centre context.

The educator's role supporting early peer relationship formation

From the United States, a recent observational study by Williams, Mastergeorge and Ontai (2010) found that, although caregivers used a range of strategies that supported infants' developing awareness of their peers, the most prevalent strategy was to reposition the infants so as to prevent conflict. A similar strategy is identified in Davis and Degotardi's (in press) interview-based study of infant educators' perspectives about peer relationships, whose reported teaching strategies revolved largely around teaching 'manners' and providing enough play materials to avoid conflicts. Together, these two studies suggest that infant pedagogy may feature a managerial focus on keeping children apart rather than providing the regular opportunities for social interactions and shared experiences from which relationships emerge. Yet, when the focus is on transition and early relationship formation, the question is not so much how do educators 'manage' social interactions between infants and toddlers, but rather, how do they *support* infants' entry into a peer group context in a way that facilitates participation in shared interactions and practices. To address this question, we turn our attention to Bella and her early experiences with both teacher and peers.

Mediating social participation

It is early days for Bella, who has been attending the nursery three days a week for just a few weeks. She has just settled after being upset when her mother said goodbye and left. Tabitha sits on the floor with her legs outstretched and places Bella on her legs, facing outwards, but leaning against her body. She picks up a book and quietly reads it to Bella, who looks around the room impassively as Tabitha reads. Millie approaches Tabitha with a monkey puppet and hands it to Tabitha, who smiles and immediately starts chanting 'One silly monkey jumping on the bed.' Millie and Bella watch the monkey together, and Millie giggles as Tabitha uses her name – 'Millie falls off and bumps her head.' Tabitha starts the rhyme again, this time substituting Bella's name. Then, noticing Noni close by, she inserts Noni's name as well. This brings Noni across to join the group where she bounces to the chant. Bella is becoming more animated and alternates her gaze between Tabitha, the monkey and Noni. She begins to look around at other children in the room, and Tabitha appears to follow her line of sight to invite other children to the game by using their names as well.

According to Howes (2009), a secure relationship with an educator provides young children with a secure base from which they can encounter and explore social relatedness with peers. In the example above, we see how Tabitha allows herself to be used as a base by Bella, whom she recognizes needs a considerable amount of personal closeness and reassurance for her at this time. When interviewed shortly after this observation, Tabitha recalled Bella and her mother's orientation visits, noting that '*She was very attached to mum. Stayed with her all the time.*' She continues, though, in her next statement, to recognize the link between relationships with significant adults and an orientation towards peers: '. . . *but she was also very interested in watching what all the children were doing, which is the next step really to being attached to mum – being into what other people are doing*'. As a result, Tabitha's teaching strategies not only responded to Bella's need for security and comfort, but also capitalized on her interest in the other children. As Tabitha explained:

She gets very close to your body . . . Then she likes to watch and listen. So that day she was facing me, but then the Friday I turned her around, and she was still on my lap, sitting on my lap, but facing the other way. Not nearly as close to me, and watching everyone else, so yeah that was quite interesting that she had slowly become more confident and comfortable.

Tabitha's description of Bella's and her own behaviours demonstrates her intent to socially orientate Bella towards others in the group and thus expand her network of relationships to include her peers. Tabitha also takes advantage of Millie's approach to inject a playful interaction into Bella's immediate experience. This strategy resonates with the case-study findings of Jung (2011), who identified caregiver playfulness as an effective means of reducing infant distress during transition. Like Tabitha, Jung describes how caregivers gradually shifted their mood from quiet comfort to joyful pleasure in response to infants' increasingly settled behaviours. Playfulness was exhibited in the form of vocal, rhythmic experiences, which, Jung argues, not only alleviated infant distress but also resulted in the shared pleasurable experiences that support infant–caregiver relationship formation. The playful interaction described above comprised a shared experience between Tabitha, Bella *and* her peers, and demonstrates how playfulness can be used to foster the beginnings of peer relationships. Bella was included, and participated in a peripheral way, in a small group game with her peers. In addition, Tabitha's encouragement and explicit inclusion of other children into the game drew Bella's focus away from the teacher to her peers, thus providing valuable opportunities to observe them, hear their names, see their playful behaviours and become comfortable in their presence.

Mediating social interaction

Tabitha begins to use the monkey puppet to chant 'round and round the garden' while moving her finger around Bella's tummy. Bella grins and allows herself to be a passive recipient of this ticking game. Millie approaches with a smile and watches a short distance away until Tabitha has finished. Tabitha asks 'Millie's turn? Come.' Then, when Millie responds to her invitation by toddling closer, Tabitha repeats the tickling rhyme with Millie. Bella looks on and chuckles with Millie at the conclusion of the rhyme. Bella then extends her finger out towards Millie, and Tabitha responds with 'More?' Millie holds out her hand, to which Tabitha responds 'It's Bella's turn?' She gently takes Bella's hand, and Bella stretches out her finger and allows her hand to be moved around Millie's palm as Tabitha says the rhyme. A moment later, Tabitha lets go of Bella's hand, yet Bella reaches to touch Millie's tummy with her outstretched finger, and watches and smiles as Millie giggles at the conclusion.[1]

Howes (2008) contends that relationships are constructed collaboratively as children, peers and caregivers share space, time, experiences and meanings. From her point of view, peer groups are cultural communities, comprising shared practices and understandings (Rogoff, 2003), so relationship formation takes place as children find ways to enter into this community of practice. In any setting, there are particular activities that have a wide-ranging appeal to infants and their caregivers. Activities such as singing and action games have long been recognized to feature heavily in interactions between infants and caregivers (Bruner and Sherwood, 1976), and in the example above, a well-known song becomes the context for Tabitha to encourage and support Bella to engage socially with her peer.

Tabitha commented about how Bella appeared to be drawn towards Millie, stating *'Bella has always been watchful of Millie, just keeping an eye on her, and it's "Oh, Millie's having fun"'* and she described how she often took advantage of Bella's interest by bringing the two young girls together to jointly participate in play activities. But the interaction between Tabitha and these two girls extends beyond a demonstration of mutual interest. It is also based on a shared understanding of the play script – of 'knowing the game' – which allows all parties to enter into an enjoyable and culturally meaningful social event (Degotardi and Pearson, 2010). The repetitive, thematic nature of the game provides a contextual frame that supports these young children's peer engagement as they re-enact individually and socially meaningful activities. Because Bella knows the game, it may well also serve as a means of reducing her uncertainty – the incorporation of a familiar ritual helping her to develop a sense of comfort and belonging with her peers in this new and often unfamiliar setting (Brooker, 2009).

Furthermore, as Brooker (2009) explains, the transition period involves changes in identity as infants come 'to understand their own separate nature and agency *in relation to* others' (p. 99, italics added). With Bella, we see how her enjoyment and knowledge of the script allows her to move from being a passive observer and recipient in a largely adult-led experience, to an active participant with her peer. Her role changes and, with this shift, she demonstrates a new-found sense of control in the situation. What results is the kind of joint participation that has the potential to become an important contextual 'meeting point' that fosters the developing relationship between Bella and Millie.

The active role of infants and their peers

So far, this chapter has focused largely on the contribution of adults and social-contextual features in supporting the transition of infants and toddlers into group-care contexts. The question remains, though, whether infants and toddlers are solely dependent on the intervention of, or support from, adults in order to relate socially with their peers. What about the contribution of the infants themselves?

A different perspective: a readiness to be social

Wittmer (2008) states that 'Babies are ready for relationships, not just with their favourite adults but also with peers' (p. 30), and thus proposes that infants have innate relational capabilities that they are motivated to use with both adults and peers from an early age. Her stance reflects a long tradition of research into early peer interactions, which has documented how infants show distinct social behaviours towards peers in the presence and absence of adults (Hay, Caplan and Nash, 2009). Despite the contention of some theories that infants' capacity for relatedness with peers is limited, others argue that infants display distinctive social behaviours that herald the very beginnings of peer relationships and that this relatedness should not necessarily be assumed to be contingent on the relationships they have with adults (Selby and Bradley, 2003). In particular, it is proposed that, in contexts where infants spend significant amounts of time together, they clearly demonstrate behaviours that pave the way for their incorporation into the social group of their peers.

In a recent review of infant peer social capabilities, Hay, Caplan and Nash make the case that rudimentary peer sociability, and therefore the foundation of peer relationships, is evident in the very first months of life (Hay *et al.*, 2009). With increasing age, infants increasingly orientate themselves towards peers in group contexts, clearly demonstrating an 'interest in peers as potential social partners' (Hay *et al.*, 2009, p. 127) that is distinct from the relationships they are developing with significant adults in their lives. In this final section, we examine how 8-month-old Matthew used these social capabilities to reach out to his peers.

Orienting and watching

Matthew is lying, head up, on his stomach on the floor. He begins to push himself along, when there is an audible scratching sound from a chair behind him. He stops, swivels 180 degrees and watches 9-month-old Jonah who is walking supported by a chair that he pushes across the floor. Rising on his hands and knees, Matthew rocks while visually tracking Jonah as he walks past. Georgia, who is sitting in a seat directly behind Matthew is also watching, and begins to bang a plastic spatula that she is holding against the seat. Matthew looks around, and begins to swivel again. Georgia observes, holding her position until Matthew is facing her. Matthew pushes himself up on to his hands to meet Georgia's gaze before swivelling again towards Jonah.

The act of watching is regarded by many as a basic indication of social attraction and interest and, thus, as an initial building block from which peer sociability can emerge (Eckerman and Whatley, 1977; Hay *et al.*, 2009). Watching and the meeting of gaze, though, can indicate more than social curiosity. In an early study of infant socially directed behaviours, Jacobson (1981) describes how many of the interactions that he observed between both familiar and unfamiliar infants often appeared to be a means of 'checking each other out' (p. 622). Within the context of transitioning into the group peer environments, watching provides infants with a means of ensuring security and of becoming familiar with the presence of multiple peers. His teacher, Tabitha, recognizing that his previous social experiences have been limited to close interactions with adults, explains his early social behaviours as follows:

. . . he doesn't seem to have that connection yet with other children. It seems to be that he's been in an adult world . . . he almost got anxious because every time he was on the floor with someone, he would be watching them.

In this way, Tabitha acknowledges the significance of watching for Matthew as a means of reducing any negative, stressful impact of his new encounters with peers.

Seeking proximity

Matthew is playing independently on the floor and Jonah, who is a short distance away, is mouthing a shiny piece of fabric. Every now and then, Matthew looks up and observes Jonah for a few seconds before resuming with his own play. Suddenly, Matthew pushes himself up on his arms, pushes with his feet and shuffles rapidly towards Jonah. As he gets close, Jonah puts down his cloth and watches Matthew approach. Matthew reaches out for a hollow wooden block on the floor next to Jonah's foot. Jonah also reaches towards it and their fingers touch momentarily. Jonah picks the block up and shakes it, making it rattle. Matthew observes this activity and then pushes on slightly to reach another block. He picks it up and, as he does so, Jonah looks at him and shakes his block again.

In an interview study of Australian infant–toddler educators' understandings of infant social behaviours, Davis and Degotardi (in press) detail that these educators described how infants would watch to learn about others' activities, explaining it as a way of learning about one another and gaining entrance into the activities of their peers. Furthermore, they described how objects often brought infants together, as mutual attraction towards the same items resulted in proximity-seeking behaviours. Matthew watched Jonah before gaining the confidence or motivation to approach. The block, as a shared focal point, brought about a brief touch, after which Matthew again watched Jonah's actions before seeking a similar object of his own. What resulted was a short episode of meeting, where these two young peers showed mutual attention to each other and ultimately engaged in a similar exploration. For Matthew, these behaviours appeared to herald a first step towards a transition from his previously adult-centred social world to one that now included an interest in becoming more close to his peers.

The examples above demonstrate how Matthew brought certain social behaviours and motivations into his new social environment. However, Matthew was not alone in contributing towards his transition into his peer community. Tabitha recalls how his infant peers were interested in this new addition to their classroom, responding in particular to Matthew's tendency to smile broadly at nearby children:

. . . he will make eye contact with a person and will acknowledge when someone looks at him with a smile. [It is] one of the biggest ways to welcome someone to come over. Like if someone's crying the child is not necessarily going to go to them, but if they're smiling it's like 'what kind of thing is he doing? I might go and join him.'

Older peers were often observed to watch Matthew closely, maybe, as Tabitha thought, because they were *'intrigued by something that small'*. Others would bend over to meet his gaze, would gently stroke his head as they toddled past, or would bring an object to put in front of him on the floor in an apparent invitation to play (Degotardi, 2011a). When considered alongside Matthew's own social overtures, it is possible to see how the efforts of his peers also made an important contribution towards Matthew's gradual accommodation into his peer community.

Some final thoughts

In concluding this chapter, we highlight two points of interest, emerging from both the excerpts and discussions. The first (recognized, in fact, by one of the parents who participated in our study, when he asked *'Why does your study end after three months?'*), is that transitions do not occur within a finite period. They merely represent the starting point of ongoing change and adjustment. This seems particularly true in relation to the relationship-based transitions described in this chapter, which are characterized by a continuous process of developing new understandings, negotiation and adaptation.

The second important point is the crucial role of early childhood educators in successfully facilitating early relationship formation during this transition, not only for children but also for their families and for colleagues within the centre. The thoughtful manner in which the early childhood educators depicted here navigated and responded to children's and parents' needs provides vital insight into this key role. Educators needed to continually update their strategies as parents and their young children entered into this new relationship-rich context. We concluded Chapter 2 with a comment on the importance of reflection and collaboration in formal settings that cater for young children. On this basis, we repeat that same suggestion here: the capacity of professionals to demonstrate a reflexive, responsive and continuously adaptable approach to relationship-building is key to achieving positive transitions in early childhood education settings.

Note

1   A version of this observation was originally published in Degotardi and Pearson (2010).

5 Relationships with and between adults: caring, learning and working together

> The key is curiosity, and it is curiosity, not answers, that we model. As we seek to learn more about a child, we demonstrate the acts of observing, listening, questioning, and wondering.
>
> Vivian Paley

Infants are born into a world structured by adults. In their earliest days, they are dependent on older community members for care, affection and attention. In the main, it is adults who shape the content of infants' days and, consequently, the kinds of experiences that make up their lives (Lamb, Bornstein and Teti, 2002). Infant and toddlers' relationship experiences with significant adults therefore constitute a central focus point in their lives, and form a foundation for both their future learning and development, and the ways that they live within and approach the world (Butterfield, Martin and Prairie, 2004; National Scientific Council on the Developing Child, 2004).

The relationships that professionals working in infant–toddler programmes have with the infants and toddlers, parents and other professionals in these settings can have a deep and lasting impact on the lives and learning of these key stakeholders. A dominant, underlying motive behind all of these relationships is, as Paley (1986, p. 127) expressed, a desire to learn more about the child and therefore be able to provide experiences that will most effectively support his/her wellbeing and learning. This aim can be achieved directly, through the interactions that educators have with the infants and toddlers in their programmes, as well as indirectly, through the professional relationships that occur between educators, their colleagues and families. As explained in Chapter 1, relationships impact on relationships, so by observing, listening, questioning and wondering about how these relationships can be understood and theorized, we gain a stronger understanding about the significance and implications of relationships with and between adults in infant–toddler programmes.

In this chapter we focus on forms and features of adult relationships within the infant–toddler classroom. We begin by outlining how infant–toddler rooms comprise a network of relationships involving adults, each of which will interact with, and impact on the others. We then discuss three main 'types' of relationship in this context: relationships between educators and parents, educators and children, and educators and their colleagues. We draw on a range of data from the *Relationship Perspectives* and the *Understanding Infants* studies to analyse the diversity and complexity of these highly significant relationships.

A 'triangle' of relationships

In the early years context, research and professional literature has predominantly explored the nature and significance of educator–child relationships, and there now exists a wealth of evidence that demonstrates the crucial role that this relationship plays in regards to the interaction opportunities afforded to very young children, as well as for long-term social, emotional and cognitive development (National Scientific Council on the Developing Child, 2004). Such research proposes that the quality of infants' and toddlers' relationships with adults has a *direct* effect on their wellbeing and development through the social, emotional and intellectual environments that educator–child relationships afford (Lamb *et al.*, 2002).

Adults, however, can also affect infants' and toddlers' lives *indirectly* through the relationships that they have with one another (Lamb *et al.*, 2002; Lewis, 2005). The nature of the relationships that significant adults have with one another forms a significant aspect of the young child's social context, as it is likely to result in a flow-on effect to the child. In an acknowledgement of the interactional nature of different relationships, Hohmann (2007) conceptualizes relationships in early childhood contexts as 'triangular,' involving a network of relationships between educator, child and parent. At various levels, the quality of adult–adult relationships will impact the emotional climate in early childhood settings, as harmony and mutual understanding, as well as stress between adults, invariably cause dynamics that can ultimately affect professional practice (Hohmann, 2007).

Research in focus: *Relationship Perspectives* and *Understanding Infants*

In this chapter, we present data from two studies to support our analysis of the different forms, features and processes related to relationships with adults in infant–toddler programmes.

From the ***Relationship Perspectives*** study we use survey and focus group data to illustrate parent and educator perspectives about the desired functions, processes and characteristics of educators' relationships with parents, infants and toddlers, and other educators. Our survey data were designed to provide insights into parent (n=200) and educator (n=71) perspectives on educator–child, educator–parent and child–child relationships through quantitative responses to an online questionnaire. The survey comprised a range of statements about different functions of educator–child, educator–parent and child–child relationships, which parent and educator respondents rated to indicate how important they felt these functions were (for more detail, please refer to Degotardi *et al.*, 2013). For each relationship type (i.e. educator–child, child–child, educator–parent) respondents were asked to provide up to five key words or phrases that they felt represented the characteristics or dimensions of an 'ideal' relationship, and also to list factors that they felt 'helped' and 'got in the way of' that relationship. We also conducted focus groups with a sample of parents and educators from three of the childcare centres based in Sydney that had provided survey data, as a follow-up to further understand some of the data emerging from this survey regarding each of the three relationship 'contexts' outlined above.

From the ***Understanding Infants*** study we present observational and interview data as the basis for our discussion of the qualities of educator–infant relatedness. In this chapter, we report on the varying ways that educators interpret infants' experiences, before meeting Denise and 15-month-old Lori to focus on the nature of their interactions as they participate together in the contexts of caregiving and play.

Parent–educator relationships

As we have discussed in previous chapters, the importance of parent–educator relationships in policies for formalized childcare and education settings is now widely acknowledged. For some time, research has demonstrated a number of benefits related to the establishment of positive educator–parent relationships in early childhood contexts. The nature of the early childhood educator's relationship with the parent not only impacts the emotional and learning climate in the classroom and at home, but also can influence the quality of relationship that the educator is able to form with the child (Owen, Ware and Barfoot, 2000; Hohmann, 2007). A strong relationship between parents and educators can be a source of social-emotional support and information for the parent, which can strengthen the relationship they have with their own child. Furthermore, in a context where educators are encouraged to work in partnership with parents to determine and deliver what is 'best' for each individual child, practitioner–parent relationships can be sites for the communication and negotiation of information about the child and home or centre experiences, thus providing a way of developing shared goals, and tailoring programmes to suit and provide for individual learning styles, temperaments and family expectations (Harrist, Thompson and Norris, 2007; Alasuutari, 2010).

In recognition of this body of research, early childhood curriculum frameworks from different parts of the world (for example, Australia's Early Years

Learning Framework, Fiji's Na Noda Mataniciva, Ireland's Síolta, New Zealand's Te Whāriki and the UK's Early Years Foundation Stage) all acknowledge the importance of families and communities in supporting children's learning and development, and call on early childhood educators to collaborate with parents and families as part of professional practice (Ministry of Education, 1996; Centre for Early Childhood Development and Education, 2006; Ministry of Education National Heritage Culture and Arts, 2008; Australian Department of Education Employment and Workplace Relations, 2009; Department of Education, 2012). However, outlining the importance of parent–educator relationships in policy documents is one thing, developing effective ways to establish and nurture such connections in real-life settings is a different matter. Of all the relationships that are formed within early childhood care and education settings, the parent–educator relationship is perhaps the most complex and fraught with confusion (Hohmann, 2007). At present, relatively little is known about what types of parent–educator relationship are preferred and/or most likely to impact positively on young children across a range of contexts.

In reality, this ambiguity is not surprising: parents bringing their young children for care and education will themselves have experienced a lifetime of socialization. The priorities and expectations that parents and educators have for children are often different, due to their differing personal and professional concerns relating to the young child, and their own caring and educating responsibilities (Hohmann, 2007). Furthermore, previous relationship experiences also come into play. Some parents may have been socialized to feel comfortable with close, intimate 'friendship'-type relationships with professionals. Others may feel more comfortable with a somewhat more detached professional 'partnership', involving formal exchange of information pertaining to their child's wellbeing. Others may yet feel reluctant to engage at all with early childhood professionals, if they themselves have been raised to defer to professional knowledge.

Various attempts have been made to define effective methods and preferred strategies for establishing relationships. One way is through understandings of the dimensions of educator–parent relationships that are, to varying degrees, desired by both adult groups. In a survey-based study of parent and caregiver perspectives on ingredients of effective relationships, Elicker and colleagues (1997) found that both parties sought confidence in the other's ability to care for and form strong relationships with the child. Collaboration was also desired, as was a sense of affiliation and caring. From our *Relationship Perspectives* survey, the key words supplied by our respondents to describe the dimensions of an 'ideal' parent–educator relationship support Elicker and colleagues' broad categories. Figure 5.1 shows, in bold capitals, the six most frequent key words that were provided by parents and educators. The size of the font illustrates the relative frequency with which

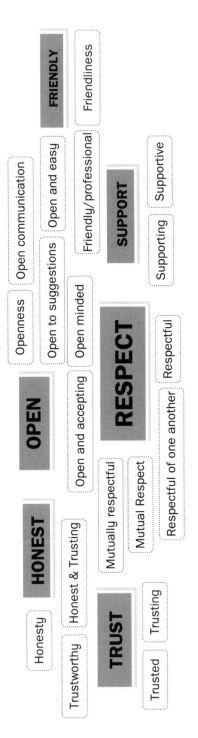

Figure 5.1 Key words and phrases used to describe the educator–parent relationship.

these words appeared in the data, with the surrounding lower-case words and phrases showing the various ways that these dimensions were referred to.

Respect, trust, honesty and openness were dominant ideas, suggesting that parents and educators want to be able to work closely together and have confidence in one another to accept and respect one another's ideas and roles. The presence of 'Support' and 'Friendly' in our data would appear to be closely affiliated with the affiliation/caring dimension that was identified by Elicker *et al.* (1997).

A different perspective: negotiating personal and professional roles

Recently, discussions around parent–educator relationships are beginning to reflect understanding that the underlying premises on which relationships are built between adults within early childhood care and education settings are highly complex. Rather than attempting to define generic strategies, or components, of effective parent–educator relationships, contemporary discussions centre more on the importance of negotiation between individual parents and their child's educator(s). As Brooker (2010, p. 194) concludes, 'The mutual and bi-directional "socialization" of children and their caregivers may no longer conform to the traditional textbook version of family and community caregiving, but to a new set of relationships in which personal and professional roles and identities need to be negotiated.' For early childhood educators and caregivers, then, navigating interactions with parents is, as Goouch and Powell (2013) point out, complex. It involves finding a point at which wider discourses about parent–educator relationships (reflected, for example, in curriculum frameworks) intersect with the individual experiences, motivations, beliefs and values of each family/parent.

Establishing shared priorities and expectations

Our own joint research was designed to explore both parent and educator perspectives on the nature of parent–educator relationships and/or partnerships in infant and toddler settings. We were particularly interested in trying to understand whether parents and educators share ideas about *how* parent–educator interactions and relationships are 'supposed' to work, and to understand what is *expected* (among parents and educators) in terms of outcomes or benefits of these relationships. Through a mix of quantitative and qualitative approaches, we found some common ideas about relationships, such as those illustrated in Figure 5.1. However, there were also some important distinctions. Priorities and expectations expressed by parents and educators in relation to parent–educator relationhips varied across settings These expectations could be seen to be influenced by an array of factors, ranging from parents' own early experiences of care/formal schooling, to regulatory policies and the unique frameworks/ philosophies within which professionals in infant–toddler programmes work.

In terms of understanding complexities underpinning professional expectations, the origins of wider discourses (in particular, recent changes in discipline-based perspectives on parental involvement) are important for highlighting the complex web of influences that have shaped both the way that parent–educator relationships are viewed, and why they are seen as so important for effective care and learning. For decades (shaped heavily by John Bowlby's (1969/2000) influential studies on maternal–child bonding), early childhood development has emphasized the critical role of early parent–child interactions in shaping young children's developmental outcomes. With the increasing use of out-of-home, formalized early care and education, subsequent research has demonstrated that supporting parent–child relationships within formalized early childhood care and education settings can also result in positive outcomes for young children. Early childhood interventions that incorporate high levels of parental involvement to support interactions between parents and young children result in positive child outcomes that are longer lasting and more effective than programmes that do not emphasize parental input (Kâğitçibaşi, Sunar and Bekman, 2001; Kâğitçibaşi *et al.*, 2009).

Based on this particular evidence base, parent–educator relationships are important because they serve the function of supporting positive parent–child interactions. This perspective is reflected in the sentiments of one of the educators who participated in our research, as she explained her rationale for establishing relationships with parents of children in her room:

Well at the moment we've ten new families that we're settling in to the room so for us it's definitely about building relationships with the families . . . just the, you know, exchange of information about their child and, you know, how they're settling in to the room as well . . . a lot of parents seemed very willing to help out and this year we just see, the children seem to have settled in a lot better too and I think it's part of the relationship that we are building up with the families.

Finding effective communication mechanisms

Alasuutari (2010) describes a more recent and slightly different set of influences that have emphasized parent involvement in early childhood care and education. These influences have a more sociological orientation and reflect broader changes in governance cultures in the 'Western', industrialized societies. She claims that public services in many contemporary societies have moved away from an assumption of power-dependency relations, towards more democratic structures ostensibly underpinned by a focus on equality and independence. According to Alasuutari, the emphasis on accountability and client-focused services in the private sector that has grown in recent decades is likely to have (1) accelerated the notion of 'partnership' between families and professional services in the provision of care and education, and (2) to emphasize the documentation of learning outcomes/experiences as a form of communication with parents in childcare and education settings.

Ironically, some of the feedback from Sydney-based parents in our Australian study suggests a possibility that some of the very policies and systems that have been designed to enhance communication between parents and educators appear to cause situations and frustrations that might result in the opposite effect. Most curriculum frameworks now place some degree of emphasis on the importance of formal communication between parents and educators, via documentation of children's learning, for example. Some centres in Sydney now communicate with families via 'soft copy' portfolios stored on USB memory sticks for reading on computers. According to some of the parents we spoke with as part of our attempts to better understand how parents and educators understand their relationships, this form of interaction is not necessarily what they expect, or feel comfortable with:

As a parent I don't want to read reams of paperwork, in fact the portfolio that they do, whilst it's lovely, they now only issue them on USB sticks and I'm not technical. I don't want to take a USB stick home. I'd much rather have the everyday update, the personal two-minute conversation and that's much better.

Interestingly, our conversations with some staff revealed similar concerns to those expressed above, regarding excessive paperwork. We took particular note of the concerns expressed by the director of one of the early childhood centres involved in our research, mainly because it resonated so well with those of the mother referred to above:

I think too one of the things that we're trying to focus on is less paperwork . . . for example, last year I had a parent come and say, 'Look, there's not much in my child's portfolio.' And I said, 'Well the documentation's there, the staff just need to print it out and put it in. However, I'm not paying these girls to sit at the computer for hours every day to write up what your child's doing. I would prefer them to be out there interacting with your child and developing a great programme for actually being with the children rather than spending all their time writing it up' . . . I think that there is still a big imbalance in a lot of centres between documentation and engagement with children [sounds of agreement] . . . More time [seems to be] spent on making the portfolios look pretty rather than actually [developing] the portfolios as a result of the interactions. And I think that's a hard balance to find.

As this excerpt suggests, our conversations with staff indicated that, while some parents may not see the need for detailed written documentation, others attach a great deal of importance to portfolios. This suggests that there may be a range of hopes and expectations among families whose children attend the same infant–toddler setting, and that there are likely to be different degrees to which these hopes and expectations are met by those of centre staff and management.

The rich conversations that we enjoyed with both staff and parents highlighted an important issue in terms of different ways in which parent–educator relationships, as well as tools to support such relationships, are viewed. Tools such as portfolios are often referred to in curriculum documents and policies as valuable for communicating children's learning and growth to parents and in building relationships between parents and educators. Our conversations with parents and educators suggest that deciding on how best to *effectively* communicate with parents, for the purposes of establishing a relationship, requires a level of understanding, on the part of staff and educators, of parents' priorities and expectations. In Chapter 3, we discussed at some length various dimensions and functions of relationships. When we apply the 'functions and dimensions' lens to parent–educator relationships, we are reminded that forming effective parent–educator relationships requires the provision of multiple opportunities for communication and interaction.

Authenticity and reciprocity

Another source of influence, in terms of promoting the importance of mutually respectful interactions between educators and parents, has been the recent push for greater attention to social justice and appreciation of socio-cultural diversity (Gonzalez-Mena, 2010). As part of this movement, greater acknowledgement of the *funds of knowledge* that parents and educators bring to their experiences and interactions in early childhood care and education settings has led to increased interest in, and appreciation of, aspects of life experience that exist outside professional and centre boundaries (Hedges, 2012). Such an approach is demonstrated by this teacher's thoughts about the necessary depth and intimacy required for 'authentic' parent–educator relationships:

It's got to be a rich relationship that's about much more than just having a magic relationship about their child's growth. It's got to be about what they like and what they do and what they've brought and what I've brought and that, like that authenticity in a relationship. And I think that that's part of the kind of seeing it as being for ever. And sometimes you never see them again but it doesn't matter . . .

The element of *caring* about and showing interest in 'the other' that is unstated and yet so evident in this teacher's depiction of parent–educator relationships is increasingly referred to as essential for effective parent–educator communication and relationship-building. Caring about what another person feels and thinks is crucial in order to facilitate the 'patient listening' that Brooker (2010) views as the foundation for respectful reciprocity. As part of the listening and relationship-building process, early childhood professionals need to be able to accept and embrace (care about) individual and unique parent perspectives on child-rearing that might contrast with their own.

The data that we present here represent only a small piece of the complex puzzle of networks and influences that we encountered in conversations with parents and educators. However, they provide glimpses of the extent to which each family and each infant–toddler setting has its own unique history and, therefore, set of priorities and expectations. Some of the parents we spoke to referred back to their own experiences of transitioning to school in explaining their hopes and expectations for children. Some of the educators used examples of families and children returning to the centre decades after 'graduation' to highlight their perspective on relationship-building; others expressed a concern with more administrative goals in establishing open communication with parents. All of which, as well as supporting the literature on relationship-building presented here, convinces us of the importance of negotiation and listening in parent–educator relationships. Mutual respect, responsiveness and reciprocity are fundamental to this process, and, as Brooker points out, 'such reciprocity may be enabled through the voicing of differences' (2010, pp. 194–195). By appreciating this complexity, and accepting this difference, we open up avenues for meaningful communication oriented towards getting to know one another better, which will ultimately support authentic relationship-building between educators and families.

Educator–child relationships

As we have seen, the quality of relationships between educators and parents has strong and various ramifications for the experiences that these adults have with young children, both in the home and centre contexts. By forming an authentic and mutually responsive relationship, parents and educators get to know the child better, both in terms of individual behaviours, experiences, styles and preferences, as well as in relation to the expectations, priorities and typical practices associated with both home and centre contexts (Alasuutari, 2010; Hohmann, 2007). This deeper knowledge creates a basis from which to interact and connect with the child, thus impacting on the relationships that are formed in both settings.

The emphasis on the quality of adult–child relationships is founded on a wealth of research that demonstrates that this relationship has a central role to play in young children's development, learning and wellbeing. Brooker (2009) draws on this extensive body of research to conclude that it is through their relationships with adult caregivers that infants and toddlers begin to develop a sense of who they are as individuals in relation to others in their world. The reciprocal interactions that form a core component of any relationship provide young children with ongoing feedback about their own behaviours, reactions, responses and intentions, all of which allow them to progressively construct an understanding of their own identity as well as the identity of others within that particular context.

Much of the existing research has been conducted from the perspective of attachment theory, and has demonstrated that close, secure attachments between very young children and their educators can have lasting impacts on their development and learning across a range of areas (see Lamb, 2005, for a review of this evidence). In Chapter 4, we examined some of the processes that are associated with the formation of attachment relationships, detailing how strategies such as sensitivity, physical availability, closeness and transitional experiences can all support the formation of emotionally and socially supportive relationships between infants, toddlers and their educators.

In this chapter, we take a different direction to consider some other, less researched kinds of relationships between educators and infants. As a starting point, we present key word data from the *Relationship Perspectives* survey. As expected, responses were varied, with more than 80 different words or short phrases listed more than once in a total of around 1,100 supplied responses. Six ideas, though, stood out, with words related to these ideas representing almost half of all responses. In Figure 5.2 we show these key ideas, using the same formatting as before to show relative frequency and associated words and phrases.

In Chapter 2 we discussed how tensions exist in relation to perceived separation of care and education, with care often regarded as a 'poor cousin' to education, with the accompanying assumption that it is something that can be provided without the need for a specialized, professional knowledge base (Rockel, 2009; Taggart, 2011). Our data, though, validate the significance of care, clearly demonstrating that parents and educators regard it as an essential characteristic of educator–child relationships. While traditional notions of care have focused around the provision of physical care, our data portray a much more complex view of what is involved. For this reason, we revisit 'care' to explore in more depth how this characteristic can be conceptualized in contemporary professional practice.

Reconceptualizing 'care'

What does it mean 'to care'? This deceptively simple question is difficult to answer, and has been the subject of much debate and discussion in recent years (e.g. Dahlberg, Moss and Pence, 1999; Rockel, 2009; Taggart, 2011). What is apparent, both in our own data and in the research literature, is that 'to care' involves teaching behaviours as well as personal and

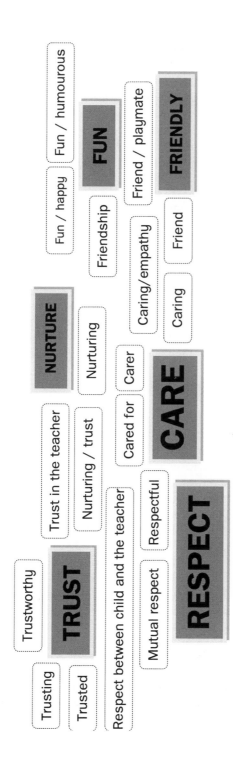

Figure 5.2 Key words and phrases used to describe the educator–child relationship.

professional dispositions that are regarded as integral to early childhood professional practice.

As we detailed first in Chapter 2, authors such as Rockel (2009) and Manning-Morton (2006) debated the idea that 'care' relates to a satisfaction of children's basic emotional and physical needs. However, the inclusion of the terms '*care for*' and '*carer*', and the presence of the key idea '*Nurture*', in our data suggests that the provision of the physical and emotional aspect of care is perceived as a desirable dimension of the educator–child relationship. The significance of this aspect of care has previously been documented by Brooker (2010), who, in her study of parents' and educators' conceptualizations of care, found that a secure, attachment-like emotional bond between young children and their educators was regarded as fundamental to children's wellbeing. On a practical basis, this relationship characteristic was strongly associated with the provision of physical care, as provided by educators during routine times such as changing, dressing and mealtimes. Our own survey results echoed Brooker's findings. When asked to rate the degree to which they agreed with certain functions of educator–child relationships, three statements – '*It is important for the educator to care for children's physical and/or health needs*', '*It is important for children to feel safe and secure around their teacher*' and '*It is important for teachers to protect and comfort children when they need this*' – attracted almost universal agreement. The practice of '*caring for*' infants and toddlers was thus held in high esteem, justifying recent calls to include care as an integral and vital aspect of the infant–toddler curriculum and pedagogy.

However, notions of care go deeper than the act of '*caring for*'. Brooker (2010) found that, if physical and emotional care was provided in a custodial or technical, 'tick-a-box' manner, parents and educators were not satisfied that this contributed to the development of close educator–child relationships. What was important was that educators '*cared about*' children, or as Brooker describes, 'a relationship of attentiveness, responsiveness and thoughtful consideration between caregiver and cared-for' (p. 193). This deeper, more emotional and heart-felt notion of 'care' was described by one of our survey parents:

My child didn't really settle in childcare until this teacher joined the class. I think the difference between her and the other teachers is that she considers what a child needs, then attends to him. Something like what a mother does. When she has tender loving care in her heart, her actions will show it, the kids feel it. The children calm down with her, as she is willing to take that extra step to attend to them. Patience is very important.

This parent identified 'loving care' as an integral aspect of what was respected in this educator's relationship with her own infant. Usually thought of in the context of close, family relationships, love is associated with the kind of deep and enduring emotional attachment that can be difficult to reconcile with a professional education and caring role, as well as possibly being perceived as a threat to parent–child relationships. According to Page (2011), though, the idea of love should be openly discussed as an important aspect of an educator's relationship with very young children. She cites Goldschmied and Jackson (2004, p. 44) to explain that 'sharing love and affection with another caregiver is not like sharing a cake where the more people there are, the less there is for each', and thus argues that 'professional love' does not need to compete with the love between parent and child, but can, instead, complement it.

Page (2011) conceptualizes professional love in a way that is consistent with many of the characteristics of care identified by our own and Brooker's (2010) research. Love, argues Page, involves respect and an empathetic commitment towards the perspective of others, which results in a deep, ethical and intellectual stance towards the children in one's classroom. The mothers in her research sought this level of commitment and involvement from their children's caregivers, but while they 'appeared to want the adults who cared for their children to love them . . . they did not always call it love' (p. 320). They sought what Page refers to as 'pedagogical loving', which embodied a professional, caring stance that was distinct from their own relationship with their child.

The uneasiness around the idea of love as part of the educator–child relationship may explain why, in our own research, the word 'love' and the associated word 'loving' were almost totally absent from the key words provided by parents and educators. Page (2011) cautions that parents want professional caregivers to love their children, 'but not too much' (p. 319). Maybe this points to why our survey respondents more readily nominated '*Friendly*' as a key word, suggesting that a concept of friendship sits more comfortably in people's ideas about infant–toddler relationships in professional contexts. In Brooker's (2010) study, educators described their relationships with infants as 'like a best friend' – someone that is always there for the children and to whom they can go for comfort, assistance and companionship. The prevalence in our own data of the word '*fun*' adds to this equation, and illustrates how the functions of educator–child relationships should extend beyond those of care and attachment to include companionship, camaraderie and playful learning (Brooker, 2009; Degotardi and Pearson, 2009; Jung, 2011). In this way, concepts of care are more holistically defined, with notions of 'caring for' and 'caring about' these very young children reflecting the distinct roles and experiences of educators and children in the context of infant–toddler settings, as well as broader societal ideas about adult–child relationships in general.

A different perspective: acknowledging and encouraging agency

While care, with all of its complexity, is undoubtedly an integral feature of the educator–child relationship in infant–toddler programmes, it is largely associated with the behaviours and attitudes of the educator. Care is something that is widely assumed to be provided by the educator and received by the child. If the educator–child relationship is solely conceptualized in this way, then the active role that infants and toddlers can play in their relationships with their educators is in danger of being overlooked.

Yet many early childhood approaches now centre on principles of active participation and agency on the part of the young child. Inspiration has been drawn from the United Nations Convention on the Rights of the Child (United Nations, 1989) to argue that even very young children have the right to be actively involved in their own experiences, learning and development, and this involves the right to express opinions, make choices and be listened to, heard and respected (Shier, 2001; Berthelsen and Brownlee, 2005). From this perspective, children are positioned as subjects: as actors and knowers who, regardless of age and capabilities, contribute towards their own learning and lived experiences in meaningful ways (Corsaro, 2005; Smith, 2011). In the context of children's relationships with educators, it is an image of a child who can contribute actively towards the features of that relationship, and who therefore exercises agency in regards to the opportunities that are afforded to him or her within the social encounters that this relationship affords.

Participatory learning

Agency is reflected through goal-directed, intentional actions and interactions, which lead to a sense of mastery and the meaningful sharing of experiences and knowledge. Child agency is central to Berthelsen and Brownlee's (2005) discussion of *participatory learning*, which theorizes children's active engagement in their own learning experiences. Berthelsen and Brownlee explain that participatory learning, at its broadest level, refers to involvement, but that this involvement can be truly realized only when there are trustful, open and reciprocal communications between educator and child. With very young children, this itself can pose a challenge, as their perceived immaturity can often be seen as an obstacle to full involvement. Maturity is therefore a factor in how participatory learning can be enacted in infant–toddler programmes:

> Recognition of the participation rights of young children involves a balance between acknowledgement of vulnerability and dependence upon adults; appreciation of children's competencies and capabilities; and encouragement, as appropriate, to allow children greater autonomy and independence.
>
> (p. 52)

In their interview study of toddler educators, Berthelsen and Brownlee (2005) describe how everyday experiences can be rich opportunities for social and intellectual engagement. Caregiving routines, they explain, provide repeated, predictable experiences that allow young children to construct knowledge of that event, regardless of their immaturity. This knowledge facilitates their participation in these routines, enabling them to increasingly exercise choice and control over time.

Research, though, suggests that young children's participation in routines is often overlooked by educators. In our *Understanding Infants* study (Degotardi and Davis, 2008), educators viewed a video-recording of a nappy-change routine in which they had both participated a short time previously, and were asked to describe and interpret that infant's involvement in the experience. We found, on the whole, that educators focused on their own caregiving behaviours when narrating the video footage, and references to the infant's participation, capabilities or perspectives were relatively infrequent. In many narratives, there was little evidence of the kind of child agency that would indicate participatory learning:

Lie her down on the nappy table. Just get her nappy 'cause she's run out. Put her down again. Give her the nappy to play with while I'm putting my gloves on. She looks at the nappy. Say the word 'nappy' to try and encourage her language. I take her nappy off. Put the clean nappy on. Sophie's looking at me. Pull up her pants, put her back down on the floor, pull up her pants. *(Degotardi and Davis, 2008, p. 229)*

In some instances, though, a distinctly different approach was taken. The following example describes how teacher Denise and 15-month-old Lori approached this familiar routine:

Denise and Lori walk into the nappy-change area together. Denise asks Lori 'Are you going to get your nappy from your bag? Or it might be in your locker.' Lori toddles over to her bag and pulls out a plastic bag. Denise states 'It's in your locker', and retrieves it as Lori continues to rifle through her bag. Lori pulls out a soft toy, and Denise asks 'What's that?' Lori looks up and holds it out, replying 'Da' to which Denise responds 'Yes – It's Panda.'

Denise places one of her hands softly on Lori's back, instructing 'Two hands' as Lori slowly and steadily climbs to the top. As she reaches the top step, Lori slips, just slightly, but Denise is there behind her to prevent against a fall and provide reassurance. Lori exclaims 'Eee! Ha' but continues to climb steadily and with confidence. Denise replies 'Hard? You hold on with two hands. You're doing well', and waits as Lori negoti-ates the final step. Denise quietly reassures Lori 'I've got you, I've got you', and keeps her hand on Lori's back as she finishes the climb, turns around and sits on the change mat. Denise acknowledges with 'That's the way. Good work!' Lori grins, says 'Down' and begins to lie down as Denise readies the nappy.

In this example, Lori makes decisions and exercises some control over her experience. Denise provides the kind of close, attentive and responsive care described in the previous section, but at the same time, she allows Lori to be a full and active participant. Lori demonstrates an impressive level of independence, drawing on her understanding of what is involved in the experience and a clear motivation to be actively involved. But there is also a degree of *interdependence* between the two in the way that they support each other in the completion of the task at hand.

The importance of balancing both independence and interdependence during routine experiences is stressed by the RIE® (Resources for Infant Educarers) approach to infant education and care. Money (2005) explains that, if infants are seen as being totally dependent on adult care during routine times, then 'adult caring will be *for* not *with* the baby' (p. 37, original italics). She stresses the need to observe closely to see what infants can do for themselves. Educators use this knowledge to carefully structure any interventions, at the same time taking a slow pace so as to give the infant plenty of opportunities to respond and participate as fully as possible. Routine events thus afford opportunities to build cooperative engagement during which both carer and child demonstrate responsiveness to, and trust in, the other. The aim of providing such close attention is to establish a relationship of mutual respect that both reflects and builds the cooperative participation of educator and young child. Brooker (2010) explains the relationship potential of experiences such as that between Denise and Lori:

> Since the care-giver is aware of caring, and the cared-for person is simultaneously aware of being cared for, a reciprocal bond develops which is mutually satisfying and mutually reinforcing: in other words, both the care-giver and the cared-for person contribute to the relationship, and both gain from it.
>
> (p. 183)

When routine, caregiving events are regarded as core experiences in an infant–toddler curriculum, permission is given to invest time and full attention to what takes place and to the learning opportunities that arise. In her interpretation of this experience, Denise explained:

Lori's very active at nappy change time. As long as you explain things, she's really good at listening and understanding . . . She's very observant of what is around her – she identifies everything in the room and she likes the one-on-one interaction, so it's nice to have a chat with her at these times.

The relationship between young child and educator thus supports social-emotional and intellectual engagement as infant and educator each respond to the other's intentions, and share thoughts and ideas. It is important to note, though, that the concept of 'caring' might vary across contexts, families and individuals. As detailed previously, in our own research, we have noted that some families may attach great importance to close physical contact in their 'care' of young children, while others may focus more on bonds that are developed through friendships or through the kinds of interactions between educators and children described here. As a consequence, the infants and toddlers themselves may approach caregiving routines with different experiences and expectations. Key to meeting these varying expectations and, in the process, establishing authentic relationships, is an interest in 'tuning in to' others' perspectives (Moore, 2007). In infant–toddler contexts, routines provide significant opportunities for educators to connect with children's thinking, not only for the purposes of sustaining a relationship, but also for learning and teaching as they afford opportunities for regular and meaningful reciprocal interactions through which new understandings can be collaboratively constructed.

Coordinating interests and intentions

As seen above, the process of responding to, and supporting, infant agency is a social one, which draws on both infant capabilities and motivations, as well as the skills and knowledge of adult caregivers and educators. This perspective reflects a commitment to the social construction of learning by placing interpersonal interactions at the centre of the learning process. The nature of these interactions will impart messages to infants and toddlers about what is expected and supported in any given context (Rogoff, 2003). Drawing on Vygotsky's 'zone of proximal development', Rochat (2001, p. 15) writes:

> Infants do not develop in isolation, and from an early age caregivers operate as reliable teachers in addition to basic care providers. Infants are supported and guided by experienced people as they learn new skills in a kind of apprenticeship.

Through interactions, shared interests and understandings can be established. As illustrated below, at its most basic, this process relies on a degree of sensitivity to the young child's interests, and a willingness to follow the child's lead during shared activities.

Denise and Lori are on the floor, playing with some toys from a toy box. Some nesting cups are scattered around and Lori picks up two of them, holding one in each hand. She says 'Cups', to which Denise nods and replies, 'There's some stacking cups.' Denise reaches in to the toy box and picks up another one – 'Here's another one.' She places her cup next to another one that is already on the floor next to Lori – 'I'll put that there' – and watches as Lori rotates her two cups in her hands.

In this observation, Denise demonstrates physical availability and contingent responsiveness, which was referred to in Chapter 4 as *behavioural sensitivity*. She allows Lori to take the lead and gently supports her explorations through the acknowledgment of her interests and the provision of resources. Such strategies support infants' and toddlers' intrinsic motivation to explore and play, and thus support naturally emerging agency (Whipple, Bernier and Mageau, 2011). By following the children's lead, educators are also able to establish joint attention with the object or objects of interest, which can pave the way for more coordinated and reciprocal interactions.

Denise watches Lori who is appearing to try to fit one of her cups inside the other. She asks 'Does it fit?' to which Lori looks up and replies 'Fit.' Denise shakes her head and looks at the cups that are on the floor next to Lori. 'Try another one. You want to try this one [points at one cup] or this one?' [points at the other]. Lori looks at the cups, then up to Denise and nods.

Denise nods encouragingly – 'I think that one might fit in there. You want to try it?' to which Lori places her cup inside one of the ones on the floor. She looks up again at Denise, who acknowledges this achievement with 'Oh, I can see!' Lori immediately picks up another cup and nests it as well. 'Very clever' says Denise, who has leant in to watch closely. 'Lucky last!' she states as Lori picks up the remaining smallest cup and nests it inside the rest – 'Oh. In we go! . . . Shall we take them out and try again?' 'Yeah' nods Lori, and she takes the smallest cup out and places it on the floor while Denise removes another – 'Yes. Maybe we can try again.'

In this observation, Denise adopts active, pedagogical roles of encouraging, supporting and assisting that are consistent with concepts of scaffolding and guided participation (Rogoff, 1998). She initiates aspects of the play and provides verbal encouragements, which seem to motivate Lori to continue in her explorations. Denise and Lori alternate between leading and following, with each play partner initiating and responding to the other's actions and words. The two appear like equal partners in a game where agency is recognized, shared and constructed through the establishment of a meaningful, collaborative activity.

According to Berthelsen and Brownlee (2005) this ability to coordinate interests and intentions lies at the heart of participatory learning:

> Participatory social knowledge construction occurs when an interaction is a shared vehicle for thought . . . .. There is true participation in the learning process when learner and teacher are mutually involved.
> (pp. 52–53)

In the example above, though, we see more than mutual involvement. Recent research has illustrated that, if shared experiences are to become a 'shared vehicle for thought', it is important that thinking processes are made explicit through language. The use of words that refer to goals, intentions and ideas has been shown to be particularly influential in children's developing understanding of their own and others' mental states and processes (e.g. Taumoepeau and Ruffman, 2008). In the example above, Denise uses words such as 'want', 'try' and 'think', and in doing so, brings otherwise internal and private mental processes out into the open to be shared between the players. When paired with their coordinated actions, the presence of such words 'gives a voice' to each player's perspectives, and therefore has the potential to both acknowledge and promote agency within communal, goal-directed and mutually responsive play experiences.

Relationships between professionals

So far, we have discussed ways in which educators, infants and toddlers and their parents can make meaningful connections that ultimately support both their relationships with one another as well as impact the learning and teaching opportunities that arise in the classroom. While Hohnman's (2007) triangle of relationships has been used to refer to relationships between educators, parents and infants, it is also vital that we recognize that the relationships that are established between educators also play a key role in supporting the well-being and learning of all of the key stakeholders in infant–toddler programmes.

In the vast majority of early childhood classrooms, adults work in teams in recognition that young children need ready access to close and responsive interactions and caregiving. These teams are usually made up of educators with different qualification levels, experience and backgrounds who are, nevertheless, required to work closely together over extended periods of time for the benefit of the children within their programmes. Given this context, strong teamwork is regarded as an important aspect of effective practice, on the basis that the demands of early childhood teaching are moderated if staff support one another and work together towards shared goals and decision-making (Papatheodorou and Moyles, 2009). In this final section of the chapter, we tackle the issue of educator professional relationships – to consider why they are important, how they can be fostered (and hindered) and the flow-on effect that relationship-based approaches can have for professional development. We begin with the question of significance.

The significance of educator relationships as an integral aspect of relationship-based approaches to teaching and learning is raised by Insley and Lucas (2009), who claim that 'relationships between adults are as important in enabling children's access to the curriculum as the adult–child relationships'

(p. 158). Insley and Lucas suggest that close and supportive professional relationships between educators will not only impact on the ways that these educators support children's development and learning, but will also influence the relationships they are able to form with the children. Staff who work closely and supportively, they argue, are able to develop a collaborative approach to the care and education of the children in their programmes, which is based on shared knowledge of each child, trust in one another's contributions, and the flexibility of roles, which allows all to work in a coordinated and supportive manner.

Data from the *Relationship Perspectives* surveys support Insley and Lucas's view. When asked to identify factors that would support or hinder their own relationships, the children's educators mentioned '*having the support from teachers*' and '*staff teamwork*' as enabling factors, while '*difficult staff*' and '*lack of enthusiasm by staff members*' were noted as constraints. Such comments reflected an awareness of the interconnectedness of different relationships, identifying that the quality of the relationships that they, as individual educators, have with their team members will have a flow-on effect to their own relationships with the children:

Working together well with my team members will help my relationship with the children because it makes the days relaxed, more fun, more enjoyable and I am able to focus more on the children than the everyday things I need to take care of.

While such comments attest to the significance of educator relationships, it is interesting to note that, when compared with research and professional literature about educator–child and educator–parent relationships, the topic of relationships between educators is rarely mentioned. Insley and Lucas (2009) lament this oversight, and state that available guidance tends to focus on clarity of roles, responsibilities and accountability, as opposed to a recognition of the deeper relationships that come into play when groups of adults work together. Greenman, Stonehouse and Schweikert (2008, pp. 133–147), for example, provide advice about developing team capacity in infant–toddler classrooms, which includes:

- assigning tasks on the basis of strengths and interests
- having role responsibilities clearly defined
- developing strong supervisory skills
- allowing for collaborative decision-making
- acting respectfully and collegially towards one's team members.

Guidelines such as these may be useful in providing frameworks for professional practice, but their focus is on role clarity and lines of responsibility rather than on supporting educator relationships. Furthermore, in its generic form, advice like this cannot take into consideration context-specific demands or pressures that will impact how staff are able to relate and respond to one another. As discussed in Chapter 2, early childhood practitioners can encounter often insurmountable challenges when faced with reconciling lists of recommended practices with the reality of their daily experiences. Such guidelines, while well-meaning and grounded in tried-and-true leadership and management principles, may also have little impact in a professional field where staff turnover is high and morale, perceived status and professional autonomy is low (Sumsion, 2005; Bradbury, 2012; Clark and Baylis, 2012). This context is described by Goouch and Powell (2013) as restricting infant–toddler educators to the kinds of traditional and often unchallenged ideologies about caregiving that were discussed in Chapter 2. Most significantly, they report that feelings of isolation, when paired with poor or absent professional development opportunities result in educators who 'teetered between mother and technician, emotional and function, without the potential for shared or co-constructed learning and development to help shape a professional "self" ' (p. 35). It is clear that such personal pressures and constraints will stand in the way of forming the kinds of collegial relationships from which close and cooperative teamwork can emerge.

A different perspective: relationship approaches to professional development

The concerns raised above suggest that ways need to be found to develop educator capacity to work with both adults and young children in team environments. This involves building a range of personal and professional attributes including credibility, trust, respect and resilience, all of which then contribute towards professional growth. A significant aspect to consider is the link between feelings of identity and self-competence and the ability to form productive and collaborative relationships with others. Papatheodorou and Moyles (2009) propose that 'Being secure in professional relationships means being secure in oneself and having a clear understating of one's own identity and self-knowledge', and progress to stress interconnections between individual and collective capacities by stating that 'One's own role also functions in itself as the basis for interactions with others' (p. 155).

Papatheodorou and Moyles (2009) thus draw attention to the connection between educator relationships and opportunities for professional growth and development. Enhancing practice involves more than the acquisition of new skills and knowledge – it also includes opportunities for educators to reflect on their own experiences, emotions and opinions in relation to others who share their concerns. While one aim may be to develop individual professional identity and capacity, the collaborative and relational nature of this approach can also serve to strengthen professional relationships. Opportunities to learn and grow in companionship with others can enhance the sense of collegiality, which can ultimately provide a secure foundation from which shared approaches to working with young children and their families can be established (Goouch and Powell, 2013).

Within the centre

Despite working within a team of educators, it has been found that infant–toddler educators experience a sense of disconnect from others within their centre. This disconnect has a flow-on negative effect on professional growth as the opportunities to share and discuss ideas, problems and solutions are limited by virtue of a real or perceived separation from others in the centre. For example, Clark and Baylis (2012) interviewed infant–toddler educators about the ways in which they perceived their own role in relation to that of educators of older children, and found that these educators identified low status and lack of visibility, both among their colleagues as well as within professional literature and development programmes, as major constraints to their practice. Clark and Baylis contend that, in order to address the flow-on effect of these perceptions to professional identity and resilience, educators need space, time and support to reflect critically on their practice and share these reflections with others.

The practice of *Reflective Supervision* is one approach that aims to provide opportunities within the workplace for those working with very young children and their families to reflect on their practice and the emotional reactions that this practice often entails. Reflective supervision entails individual or small groups of educators meeting regularly and working in partnership with a supervisor or mentor to explore work challenges. These discussions particularly focus on relational aspects of their work including relationships between infants, parents, educators, managers, and broader social and/or cultural forces (Weatherston, Weigand and Weigand, 2010). Educators are also prompted to consider the interconnectedness of all relationships within the workplace, reflecting on how the nature of each relationship will impact others in the workplace. Discussions are based on principles of respect, openness, acceptance and confidentiality, with the understanding that self-awareness, and an acceptance of intense and often negative emotions are important contributors to professional growth. Supervisors allow the expression of opinions and feelings without judgement or intervention, allowing the practitioners themselves to lead the discussions, work through challenges, propose solutions and gain new insights.

Emde (2009) identifies a willingness to participate in continuous learning and improvement as a core commitment of a reflective supervision approach. Learning is ongoing and transformative, with new understandings emerging through a sharing process. It is also collaborative, as individuals gain support from others with similar concerns and learning from others' perspectives and experiences. Weatherston and colleagues (2010) acknowledge that the success of reflective supervision in enhancing professional capacity is difficult to measure, as flow-on effects from increased self-awareness and acceptance can cause periods of disorientation as well as increased confidence. They recount, though, informal observations that practitioners who participated in reflective supervision discussions with colleagues over extended periods of time reported an enhanced commitment to working together and developing deeper collegial relationships. Encouraging evidence for the impact on educators' broader relationships network was found by Virmani and Ontai (2010) in their study into the effects of reflective supervision on professional practice with infants and toddlers. These researchers found that those who engaged in regular reflective supervision sessions showed greater gains in their insightfulness and acceptance of the infants' intentions and perspectives. Given that research has demonstrated links between this kind of insightfulness and caregiver sensitivity in both home and early childhood centre contexts (Koren-Karie *et al.*, 2002; Degotardi and Sweller, 2012), it would seem that supported opportunities to reflect on relational aspects of early childhood work may well have a flow-on effect to the relationships between young children and their educators, as well as between the educators themselves.

Beyond the centre walls

While reflective discussions in the workplace form an essential aspect of professional growth, externally provided professional learning programmes are more readily recognized as an integral means of supporting the day-to-day practice of early childhood educators. Traditional approaches have concentrated largely on workshop- or lecture-style delivery of knowledge content, but programmes are now emerging that involve a longer-term commitment of educators during which they acquire new theoretical knowledge and actively explore how this can be applied in their setting. As with the *Reflective Supervision* model described above, many of these programmes aim to provide opportunities for reflective engagement, during which educators think critically about how their beliefs, experiences and reactions to new ideas contribute towards their evolving practice and the ways that they conceptualize the experiences of the children with whom they work.

A feature of these extended professional learning programmes is that they do not treat learning as an individual process, but instead provide opportunities for groups of educators to come together to learn about and then discuss and debate new ideas and experiences. Change is not only based on the acquisition of knowledge, but also on a deep consideration of how that knowledge relates to the perspectives of self and others, as well as the constraints and opportunities afforded by the educator's professional context. These relationship-based programmes aim to enhance the quality of curriculum and pedagogy by providing opportunities for educators to collectively reflect on the multiple perspectives afforded by evidence-based practice and practice-based evidence.

The enhancement of professional practice and identity occurs through an active engagement and negotiation with traditional and contemporary ideologies, as well as with the points of view of children, educators, families and communities (Osgood, 2010; Pirard and Barbier, 2012). This view provided impetus for the 'Baby Room' project (Goouch and Powell, 2013), during which educators from 25 English infant–toddler rooms were provided with regular face-to-face and online meeting spaces to discuss their practice and challenges in the field. Although the educators often expressed disheartening views about a perceived lack of autonomy, support and professional respect, the researchers also painted a more optimistic picture about how the professional networks that were built during the course of the project enabled educators to critically examine their ideas and practices. Regular discussion meetings and the accompanying professional and collegial support extended the educators' knowledge of their role and the children, as well as increased levels of confidence and pride in the significant role that they play in the lives of the children and families in their centre.

Similar findings are reported by Degotardi, Semann and Shepherd (2012), who implemented a practitioner inquiry project that aimed to encourage infant educators to challenge, reflect on and change elements of their practice. Meeting regularly for professional workshops and discussions over a six-month period, interview comments during and after the project demonstrated that a deepening understanding of infants' learning and development was being applied to their curriculum and pedagogy. Of equal importance was evidence that their professional identity was strengthened through their participation in the programme with comments like '*little by little I am making changes*' and '*the experiences I offer are more thought out from use of my own imagination*' suggested an increased confidence in their own professional knowledge and capabilities. However, it was the collegial approach that was identified as a driving factor behind the change. Statements such as '*I liked how it was not just talking, it was sharing ideas*' and '*It was being in the room with colleagues. Coming together and getting to know people*' once again reinforce the significance of a dialogic, relationship-based approach where educators collaboratively constructed new understandings.

Some final thoughts

This chapter has presented a wide range of issues to consider in conceptualizing and understanding the various relationships between adults that impact on children's experiences in infant–toddler programmes. With regard to parent–educator relationships, we find that mutuality is key: knowing one another's priorities and expectations, and using this knowledge to build effective communication mechanisms. In building enjoyable, two-way learning relationships with children, we find that educators need to be able to develop emotional and intellectual connections with the children in their care, as well as fulfilling purely physical care needs. Finally, we acknowledge that, for all this to happen, educators themselves must be provided with opportunities to share ideas, spend time reflecting about their professional lives and, ultimately, care about their work.

While the issues may differ across each of the three relationship contexts covered here, we would argue that, taken together, they highlight a key important message: that relationship-building involves a complex, yet exciting, process of learning about 'others', be they infants/toddlers, parents, grandparents, other caregivers, colleagues and other key stakeholders. Carter and Curtis (1998) sum this up beautifully, so we use their words to complete this chapter:

> To build a group culture and a sense of community, we need to know who we are and why we are here, and to begin to discover who we can be together.
>
> (p. 85)

6   Relationships with peers: togetherness, cooperation, friendship and belonging

Stand aside for a while and leave room for learning, observe carefully what children do, and then, if you have understood well, perhaps teaching will be different from before.

Loris Malaguzzi

For some time, it has been noted that research about infant and toddler relationship worlds has focused most strongly on the relationships that they have with significant adults (Selby and Bradley, 2003; Wittmer, 2008; Degotardi and Pearson, 2009). While adult–child relationships are undeniably a powerful force in children's lives, the observation that increasing numbers of very young children spend significant periods of time in group-care settings has led to a growing awareness of the need to learn more about infants' and toddlers' peer relationships. In the quote above, Malaguzzi (1998, p. 82) challenges educators of young children to become perceptive about the active role that children play in shaping their own experiences, learning and development. His call, now reflected in many contemporary early childhood texts and policy documents, is for educators to attend to young children's motivations, abilities and strengths, and to use this knowledge as a starting point when determining teaching practice (Wittmer, 2008).

Malaguzzi is quick to emphasize that this approach does not discount or devalue the role of the professional educator. Instead, he draws attention to a dynamic relationship between learning and teaching that requires educators to pay close attention to children's capabilities and contributions. He claims that, while approaches to learning and teaching often place great emphasis on teaching strategies, if educators 'stand aside for a while' new learning possibilities are identified and created as children's agency and social participation are brought to the fore. Stating that 'we tend to only notice things that we expect' (p. 84), Malaguzzi argues that close, intentional observation of children can provide surprising insights into the inner resources and personal agency that these young children bring to any learning context.

In this chapter, we follow Malaguzzi's advice, shifting attention away from the topic of educator–infant relationships to focus on the nature of infants' and toddlers' relationships with one another. We begin by reviewing evidence that demonstrates the social competencies of infants and toddlers, as it is these capabilities that lay the foundation for the social interactions from which relationships are formed and maintained (Hinde, 1997; Hay *et al.*, 2009).

Turning the spotlight on the social capabilities of infants

Despite the suggestion that notions of the 'solitary infant' remain a common feature of early childhood professional thinking (Degotardi and Pearson, 2010; Salamon, 2011), empirical evidence of infants' and toddlers' social competence with similar-aged peers has existed for some decades. Early studies in laboratory and naturalistic settings demonstrate that, during their first year, infants show a distinct interest in infant peers (Jacobson, 1981; Hay, Nash and Pederson, 1983). Within their first six months of life, infants look at their peers, participate in mutual gaze and direct smiles, and vocalize with one another (Vandell, Wilson and Buchanan, 1980). With developing maturity, interactions become increasingly responsive, involving reciprocal touching and imitative behaviours and, as they begin to crawl, infants approach, follow and reach for one another (Eckerman and Whatley, 1977; Vandell *et al.*, 1980). While studies of infant social capabilities indicate that early social overtures tend to be fleeting, socially directed behaviours become increasingly frequent and longer in duration as toddlers begin to reciprocate and coordinate their actions with those of approaching peers (Meuller and Brenner, 1977; Howes, Matheson and Hamilton, 1992). Toddler social overtures have been observed to include the giving, taking and showing of objects, and an increasing occurrence of physical contact, vocalizations and gestures (Finkelstein *et al.*, 1978; Musatti and Panni, 1981; Brownell, 1990).

The findings of these early studies have been reinforced by more recent observational research in early childhood settings. Shin (2012), for example, observed five 9- to 23-month-old infants to examine how they used their emerging social-communicative skills. Among other capabilities, Shin describes how these infants sought and followed one another's gaze, pointed in order to direct attention and request objects, smiled in response to one another's communicative attempts, and imitated joyful play actions. Similar social behaviours were observed by McGaha, Cummings, Lippard and Dallas (2012) during their practitioner inquiry project on ways to foster infant and toddler social interactions and relationships. These authors made simple modifications to their room structure, routines and experiences, with the aim of allowing older toddlers to interact freely with infants. They noted that the infants and toddlers watched, smiled at and touched one another, and showed clear interest in one another's activities. Interactions were spontaneous and occurred without adult assistance, prompting the authors to note that 'the children showed an ability to engage independently that amazed the teachers' (McGaha *et al.*, 2012, 'Spontaneous interactions', para. 2). As Malaguzzi (1998) claimed, it appears that when educators afford themselves the opportunity to observe young children's capabilities, they indeed often discover strengths and capabilities that are in danger of being overlooked if attention is paid only to infants' interactions with educators.

Infants in groups

While it is important to recognize individual social capabilities such as those described above, Selby and Bradley (2003) argue that an appreciation of infants' relationship worlds needs to extend beyond an analysis of individual contributions. They state that 'Functioning as a member of a family, a community, a school class, a sports team, a business or a government is central to what it means to be human' (p. 216), and claim that any understanding of social capabilities must entail an appreciation of what it means to exist with, and relate to, *multiple* others within any given social group. With particular reference to the peer culture in group care settings, Selby and Bradley claim that, in 'being able to recognize infants as group members, we are better able to think how to enhance the quality of their group living' (p. 217). It is through this appreciation that those working with young children are provided with a theoretical basis from which to support group-generated companionship, identity and belonging.

Research in focus: *Relationship Perspectives*

In this chapter we examine the characteristics and significance of peer relationships, with a particular focus on the group nature of infant–toddler early childhood and care settings. The data presented are derived from the *Relationship Perspectives* toddler-room case study, the method of which was described in Chapter 3.

Here we use observations of many of the children from the same toddler class of 15- to 30-month-old children as well as the perspectives of these children's educators and their parents. In doing so, we explore the forms and functions of peer relationships in that classroom from theoretical as well as practice-based perspectives. We pay close attention to the real-world meaning of these relationships from the perspective of the child, their educators and parents. Together, these multiple perspectives provide insights into the individual, social and cultural forces that function to support a range of early peer relationships.

Togetherness

Selby and Bradley's (2003) focus on group dynamics is reflected in the concept of 'togetherness' as conceptualized by Van Oers and Hännikäinen (2001). 'Togetherness' is defined as the 'tendency of forming and maintaining a group' (p. 102), and Van Oers and Hännikäinen link the feeling of togetherness with social-emotional connectedness, a shared existence and a sense of belonging. They further explain togetherness as a 'quality of a social activity' (p. 105) that participants are jointly motivated to establish and maintain. This approach calls for attention to be paid to the lived reality of children's social relatedness with their peers. As Wittmer (2008) explains, it is important to 'turn the lens to understand peer interactions from the children's viewpoint, to understand their goals and strategies and how they are experiencing the moment' (p. 6). Similarly, Singer and De Haan (2007) point to infants' and toddlers' curiosity in, and motivation to interact with others, to argue that they are 'agents in creating togetherness' (p. 298). A focus on participants' vested interest thus reinforces the significance of the functional approach to relationships introduced in Chapter 3. It also, though, requires us to think beyond the purpose of the relationship for any individual to instead consider the relevance of that shared activity for all involved.

Care and affection

A fundamental premise of togetherness is that there is social-emotional value to living closely and harmoniously with one's community members (Van Oers and Hännikäinen, 2001). Group membership provides opportunities for friendships and bonds to be formed, and for individual needs to be perceived and met by others in the group. The act of caring for others has been regarded as a hallmark of what it means to be a human, and lies at the core of pro-social behaviour (Brownell and Kopp, 2007). While we discussed concepts of care in previous chapters, we now explore yet another feature of this multidimensional behaviour. Caring demonstrates a level of empathetic concern – of feelings of tenderness towards the needs or distress of others. As such, the ability to care and 'feel for' the other is arguably one of the building blocks of togetherness, allowing individuals to acknowledge and respond sensitively to others in the group (Rochat, 2009). Although the social capabilities of infants and toddlers have, in the past, been overlooked (Degotardi and Pearson, 2010), recent evidence demonstrates the early emergence of expressions of care and concern (Davidov *et al.*, 2013). For example, empathetic concern has been inferred from observations of young toddlers who demonstrate an awareness of peer distress through facial expressions and physical actions such as patting, stroking or by the gifting of toys (Rayna, 2001). As evidenced below, concern for others can extend beyond responding to obvious distress, to a consideration of another's particular needs:

It is early afternoon and the children have just woken from their afternoon nap. Most have got up from their beds, but 17-month-old Moira, who is relatively new to the centre, is just stirring. As she wakes, Moira lies quietly on her bed and looks around expression-less. Two-year-old Ned notices that Moira has woken, and walks closer to her with his head to one side. He then turns and collects her water bottle from a nearby table and takes it across to her bed. Ned sits on the bed next to her and puts the bottle by the bed where she can reach it. As the observer looks across, Ned gestures towards Moira, and pats her gently as she lies quietly.

While togetherness is regarded as a feature of collective activity, Van Oers and Hännikäinen (2001) recognize that certain individual developmental achieve-ments and capabilities contribute towards its establishment. By collecting Moira's drink bottle and gently patting her, Ned's actions suggest a developing awareness of her unique feelings and requirements. Rayna (2001) associates this achievement with infants' developing appreciation of others' minds because acts of caring draw on toddlers' cognitive capacity to differentiate their own feelings and perspectives from those of their peers. As Brownell explains, it is this awareness that 'enables them to empathise more accurately with another's feelings and needs in different situations, and their efforts to help become more effective' (p. 139).

Such expressions of care in toddlerhood can be fleeting, occurring only when children are brought together by a perceived need. Once that need is satisfied, the motivation to remain together may pass. More enduring feelings of togetherness involve children's desires to establish proximity to other group members, both physically and emotionally. Hännikäinen (1999) describes how 5-year-old children use bodily expressions, such as touching and hugging, to demonstrate closeness and affection, referring to such behaviours as a demon-stration of a 'friendly attitude' (p. 23). As the following observation shows, it is during toddlerhood that children begin to explore and construct understand-ings about proximity and affection.

Twenty-month-old Ellen has approached 18-month-old Liesel. She is standing just to one side of Liesel, but bends slightly to look into Liesel's face and utters 'Wanna cuddle? Wanna cuddle?' Liesel responds with 'Yes.' Both girls turn to face each other with arms out and slowly wrap their arms around each other's necks. They hold this cuddle stance for a moment before Ellen moves, causing both of them to lose their balance and tumble sideways to the floor. Both girls roll to a sitting position and look at each other with serious expressions. Liesel touches her head, indicating that she may have bumped it as she fell. Ellen looks up at the observer with a look of uncertainty, and then back at Liesel – reaching out to touch her head, saying 'Fall down.'

The significance of hugging, as an expression of affection, has been noted by a number of researchers of both older and younger children (Hännikäinen, 1999; Engdahl, 2012). Consistent with Ellen's actions, Engdahl describes hugging as one of a series of behaviours in which children seek out and show affection towards a chosen peer. Young toddlers have been observed to be intentionally gentle when touching and stroking younger peers (Degotardi, 2011a; McGaha et al., 2012), but hugging requires a mutual participation of both peers. Liesel's willingness to be part of Ellen's embrace appears to demonstrate mutual recognition and a shared desire to establish closeness. This element of reciprocation is identified as significant by Engdhal, who suggests that such behaviours indicate the very beginnings of friendship.

Liesel's and Ellen's actions also draw attention to the significance of certain acts of affection within the wider socio-cultural context of the classroom. Describing similar acts of affection and care, Rayna (2001) claims that toddlers are active in their efforts to 'construct and reconstruct behaviours that they have observed in others' (adults') repertoires or that they have been (or are) the object of' (p. 113). When this observation was discussed with educators, Hasumi and Min-Jee, they suggested that Ellen may have been reproducing an experience that she herself often enjoyed with the centre staff:

Min-Jee: Liesel is a good cuddler . . . I say, 'Give me a cuddle.' She comes, and goes 'Yay!'
Hasumi: So it's part of her day – to have the cuddle.

Like expressions of care, the display of physical affection among peers has also been linked to developing empathy, which, while indicative of toddlers' developing social-intellectual capabilities, can also be situated within a broader social context. As Hasumi explains:

Sometimes we give cuddles if the children look sad, or not happy . . . So Ellen is back again, like copying what we are doing. Like, 'Ah, Liesel looks alone, maybe it would be nice to have a cuddle.'

Encounters like the one between Ellen and Liesel also highlight opportunities for children to develop social intelligence through the direct experience of the social and emotional consequences of such interactions. In a rich portrayal of the social play interactions of young toddlers, Engdahl (2011) describes how the children would frequently stop during boisterous play and look at one another as if to gauge others' reactions. She refers to these breaks in the play as 'moments for taking the perspective of others' (p. 1432), a sentiment echoed by teacher Cathy, who attributes this meaning to Ellen's reaction after the fall:

It's quite interesting that they fall over and then I suppose Ellen looks at you to see what you're going to say. Because I suppose when it's happened before, maybe she's observed people saying 'you need to be gentle' . . . And then I suppose by looking back at Liesel and saying, 'Fall down', she's trying to, not say sorry, but maybe it was an accident or she's saying it in her own way to make her better.

Cathy's interpretation demonstrates her awareness of how infants and toddlers draw on one another's reactions as a form of emotional reassurance. It also highlights how such interactions, and the participants' reactions to these interactions, provide children with immediate feedback about which behaviours are regarded as acceptable and unacceptable by other members of the group. In the example below, we see another spontaneous expression of affection between slightly older children that did not progress as smoothly as the instigator, 30-month-old Ahmed, may have liked:

Ahmed's father has just arrived to collect him. As he is readying to leave, he moves towards 32-month-old Holly with his arms outstretched and says 'Kiss!' Holly turns and runs away laughing and Ahmed takes off in hot pursuit. Holly suddenly stops laughing and with a concerned look on her face, runs towards an educator and takes refuge behind her. The educator intervenes and suggests that Ahmed just says 'Goodbye', which he does. Holly watches Ahmed as he walks towards the door, and notices a feather a short distance away. She rushes to pick it up, and turns to the educator: 'This is Ahmed's feather!' She races after Ahmed and catches up to him: 'Ahmed – I found your feather!' Ahmed stops and takes the feather from her and they both grin at one another. Holly then runs back into the playground, with a call of 'See you Ahmed!'

Although Holly was initially unsure about how to respond to Ahmed's expression of affection, this episode draws attention to how relationships involve a sense of commitment that can transcend momentary challenges and difficulties. Expressions of care and affection may originate from individual developmental capabilities or social practices, but there also needs to be a 'motivation to care' (Davidov *et al.*, 2013, p. 129). In this case, the motivation is attributed by Cathy to the strength of the relationship between these two young peers:

It didn't turn out how Ahmed wanted it to turn out. But by giving the feather back to Ahmed, Holly's sort of saying 'Well, alright?' kind of thing. How can I say it, it's sort of like a peace offering like, 'Okay I didn't want the kiss, but I still love you.'

Holly's response demonstrates that the motivation to maintain a relationship can be as much of a driving force behind togetherness as the desire to jointly participate in any discrete activity.

A sense of 'us'

A central aspect of togetherness relates to a feeling of shared existence that arises from the establishment of mutual interests, concerns and activities. When togetherness is achieved, the meaning of any action or activity transcends individual experience; meaning is shared between group members and is therefore experienced in the collective (Hännikäinen, 1999; Van Oers and Hännikäinen, 2001). The discovery of similarity or sameness has been observed to be an 'experiential glue' that brings and keeps children together (Hännikäinen, 1999; Engdahl, 2011). It is an establishment of common ground – the joint experience of interests, ideas and actions – that supports feelings of affiliation and belonging and, ultimately, a sense of 'us'.

Nineteen-month-old Lorna is playing by herself with a basket of puppets, when she is approached by 18-month-old Melanie, who has found a short piece of string. Melanie holds the string out towards Lorna, and as she does so, utters 'Like it? Like it?' Lorna looks up and smiles, but returns to her puppets. Melanie moves away briefly to two other children and holds out the string to them, stating 'Look. Like it? Like it?' The two boys do not respond, so she moves back to Lorna, holding out the string yet again. This time Lorna takes it from her with a broad grin, and says 'I like it!' Melanie retreats slightly and grins broadly as she watches Lorna, who is now stretching the string in her hand and repeating 'I like it. I like it!'

In a Dutch case study of the language interactions of one preschool-aged child, De Haan and Singer (2001) found that the establishment of common ground emerged as a significant theme in day-care-centre interactions. In their study, the explicit identification and labelling of sameness featured strongly, and commonality was a strong feature of shared presence and developing peer relationships. The example with Melanie suggests that a desire to establish common ground can be present in much younger children. While sameness was not explicitly labelled, Melanie seems to be gauging the reaction of the other children to determine whether a shared preference or interest can be found. Her obvious pleasure, on Lorna's uptake and confirmation of this interest, highlights the emotional aspect of togetherness. In particular, it suggests that toddlers actively seek to establish emotional affiliations with their peers (Hännikäinen, 1999), and illustrates how very young children initiate and respond to invitations to be included in others' experiences.

Playful actions and activities have been identified as providing rich contexts for social interactions and relationship-building (Løkken, 2000; Degotardi and Pearson, 2010; Engdahl, 2011). Hännikäinen (2001) argues that playful activities draw children together to participate in group experiences that afford opportunities for the collective expression of fun and excitement. Singer and De Haan (2007) define certain aspects of toddler joint play as 'emotional dramatic activities' (p. 288), which involve repetitive physical activities such as running, chasing and jumping. This type of shared experience, commonly observed in the *Relationship Perspectives* study, is exemplified in the example below:

> Holly and 2-year-old Alistair have each claimed possession of two wheelbarrows in the outside playground. Holly has been pushing her wheelbarrow from one side of the playground to the other, closely followed by Alistair. As she pushes, Holly frequently checks over her shoulder, as if to see if Alistair is still following. The pace begins to quicken, and the running and pushing to and fro is accompanied by frequent laughter as the barrows bump into each other. After around five minutes of this increasingly boisterous activity, Holly pushes her wheelbarrow up a sloped path, turns and waits for Alistair, still following, to join her. She pushes and releases her wheelbarrow, and both children squeal as it rolls down the slope. Alistair immediately does the same with his barrow.

Hännikäinen (2001) states that a simple desire to have fun is a driving force behind young children's motivation to play together. Holly and Alistair are clearly enjoying each other's company, and their increasing gleeful exuberance demonstrates the joy and excitement that is achieved through their shared activity. The presence of laughing, squealing and giggling is associated with a toddler play style, which Løkken (2009) refers to as representing 'their *mood* for playing' (p. 37, original italics). Løkken draws attention to the physicality of such experiences by stating that very young children 'find a multitude of means to *do* common activities' (p. 36, original italics). Imitation and repetition of simple physical actions are indicative of this play style. As Alistair closely follows Holly, his behaviour can be interpreted as imitative of her movements and actions, and it is clear that his desire to do what she is doing brings and keeps the two children together (Engdahl, 2012). Holly's frequent looking back suggests that she is concerned about whether Alistair has caught on to the essence of her play, and demonstrates how the simple, thematic content supports the establishment and continuation of shared activity between peers (see also Chapter 4 for a discussion of this feature in educator-mediated peer interactions). Thyssen (2010) refers to this structure as allowing children to easily 'capture each other's ideas' (p. 594), enabling a sharing of experiential meaning, which ultimately permits the coordination and elaboration of play actions between players. It is this ability to coordinate actions that signifies individual children's entry into the existing peer culture (Brownell, 1990), as well as their collective ability to reproduce and produce actions that contribute towards communal life experiences (Corsaro, 1994; Thyssen, 2010).

A sense of humour

In the same way that joy acts as an emotional motivation for peer play, children also feel and construct togetherness by creating and reacting to humorous acts. Loizou (2007) suggests that humorous acts constitute a distinct type of toddler play. Humour, she contends, requires children to create, perceive and respond to incongruities as they play with one another's ideas and expectations. Humorous acts occur in a number of play contexts, including physical play, play with materials and language play, and toddlers create and find humour in distinct ways depending on the style of play. In the next observation, we observe some of these strategies as Alistair and his younger peer, Annie, engage in a typical humorous exchange:

A large plastic tub, from which foam blocks have been tipped out, has been placed in the middle of the classroom floor. Alistair has climbed into the tub and 20-month-old Annie approaches. After looking at Alistair for a few seconds, Annie picks up two foam blocks and places them in the tub. Alistair responds with an exaggerated, high-pitched 'Oh! Thank you!' Annie grins and picks up two more blocks and drops them into the tub. Alistair again replies 'Oh! Thank you!' and this game continues, with Annie's movements and Alistair's response becoming more animated and exaggerated each time. Both begin to laugh and squeal as the blocks are dropped in and Alistair humorously responds. As the play becomes increasingly excitable, Annie brings over two more blocks but, instead of dropping them into the tub, she tosses them over Alistair's head to the other side of the room. She squeals with laughter, but this time Alistair remains expressionless. Annie stops laughing, looks at Alistair, and then calmly walks over to retrieve the blocks. She receives the familiar 'Oh! Thank you!' when she drops them into the tub, and the game resumes.

Loizou (2007) defines toddler humour as a blend of creativity and social interaction during which young children use their bodies and voices to turn play activities into humorous events. Alistair's exaggerated *'Oh! Thank you!'* is an example of how young children use words and sounds to create humorous situations, the silliness of which is appreciated by themselves and their peers. Laughter expresses camaraderie and enjoyment (Hännikäinen, 2001), and also reinforces the play and invites its continuation and escalation (Engdahl, 2011). Annie's repeated block-throwing action illustrates that young children not only find humour when actions are incongruous, but also when they match their expectations. As Singer and De Haan (2007) state, 'Maybe children laugh because the fulfilling of a prophesy leads to a feeling of agency and empowerment' (p. 290). However, humorous events also involve testing the limits of the play. When Annie tossed the blocks over Alistair's head, Alistair's instant withdrawal of social reinforcement appears to provide a strong message about what he regarded as acceptable and unacceptable play behaviours. Their teacher, Cathy explains:

Alistair didn't respond at all. He just went, 'I'm not going to say thank you to that.' She didn't follow the rules.

Accordingly, shared humour affords instant feedback about boundaries, and thus provides children with first-hand experience of the moral and social expectations of other group members.

A different perspective: engaging with minds

As children mature and gain increasing social experience with significant adults and peers, their understanding of the perspectives that drive their own and others' actions increases. Often referred to as children's *theory of mind*, this form of social understanding allows children to make inferences about the feelings, needs, wants, knowledge and opinions of others, and use these inferences to make sense of others' behaviours. Their developing social understanding enables children to engage with others on a psychological level to structure their interactions around both physical and mental actions. It is through children's developing ability to consider the mind that interactions become increasingly coordinated and cooperative (Carpendale and Lewis, 2006). In other words, during their social interactions with others, children not only express their own minds, but perceive and respond to the minds of others.

Cooperation and negotiation

A large body of research exists to show that infants begin perceiving, engaging with and responding to the mental lives of others within their first year of life, with an increasing awareness of others' emotions developing across the toddler years (Brownell and Kopp, 2007). As discussed earlier in this chapter, these developmental capabilities allow children to perceive and respond empathetically to others' needs and feelings. During toddlerhood, children also show increasing awareness of others' intentions – their wants, goals and plans. As motivational forces, intentions cause us to act with purpose, resulting in what Reddy (2008) describes as an 'openness – an incompleteness – . . . which invites participation from others' (p. 162). She explains that, during interactions, intentional actions often elicit a reaction in another; for example, the reaching hand provokes the other to give, or striving persistence is recognized with an offer of assistance.

Making concessions

It is through the ability to express, perceive and respond to one another's intentions that young children begin to coordinate their behaviours with others in order to establish and maintain group play (Brownell, Ramani and Zerwas, 2006).

Episodes of cooperation come about when children share intentions and establish joint goals. As we will see in the examples below, things do not always go smoothly, as individual intentions may clash and require negotiations and resolutions. However, Carpendale and Lewis (2006) stress that 'Cooperation does not necessarily refer to harmonious interaction but rather to interaction among equals who therefore feel obliged to explain their positions and understand other people's views' (p. 247). In the following observation, we see this process in action as 18-month-old Harry and 22-month-old Lia come together to play.

Lia has collected a large fabric wall-hanging, which comprises a number of felt faces that can be placed into matching coloured pockets. She puts the wall-hanging on the floor and takes four of the faces out of the pockets. Harry approaches and sits next to her. Lia frowns slightly and holds the faces closely in her lap.
Harry: 'I want.'
Lia does not respond, but when Harry holds out his hand, she allows him to take three of the faces. Lia watches as Harry places two faces into the pockets. She then points at another pocket, and Harry immediately places his last face into that pocket. Harry then moves towards Lia and holds his hand out towards the remaining face. He moves to take it, but Lia holds on to it tightly, moving back slightly and asserting 'No!'
Harry stops, and looks to one side: 'I have it?'
Lia does not move. Harry then places his hand on an empty pocket. 'Here. In here. Put it here.' He then watches as Lia moves and places the remaining face into the pocket.

Brownell and colleagues (2006) argue that that 'Toddlers' nascent understanding of goals and intentions is put to a stringent test in exchanges with one another' (p. 816), and in the episode above we see how toddler peer interactions often involve the communication, challenging and negotiation of individual wants and goals. Lia's initial defensive stance suggests that she interprets Harry's initial approach as his intention to take the faces from her. However, when Harry asserts his want, Lia accommodates to his request and her provision of assistance allows Harry to complete his intended action. Lia's concession, though, has a limit, and their clashing intentions at this point could easily have resulted in conflict. However, in a move reminiscent of Van Oers and Hännikäinen's (2001) contention that an important element of togetherness revolves around maintaining harmonious relationships among players, the initial roles swap as Harry accedes to Lia's desire and assists her to complete the task. This ability to compromise demonstrates how very young peers can capably coordinate one another's actions and intentions in order to maintain the experience (Brownell *et al.*, 2006; Shin, 2012). It also provides an example of how cooperative play, where shared wants and goals are established and enacted, begins in toddlerhood as young children successfully negotiate one another's intentions (Hay *et al.*, 2009).

Keeping the peace

Children do not always comply with their peers' intentions so readily. As seen with Lia and Harry, the expression of intent involves an individual assertion that acts as an instruction to the other. Compliance is not compulsory, and the assertion of one's individual intention over that of the other can result in opposition and power struggles.

Ahmed, Robert (28 months) and Harry are playing in the sandpit. Ahmed has managed to make a perfectly formed bear-shaped sandcastle with a sand mould.

Ahmed [to Harry]: 'Harry. Don't bump this' [pointing at his bear].

Harry looks at him seriously and pushes a truck towards the bear.

Ahmed: 'Don't bump it Harry – no!' but Harry rolls his truck over the bear.

Ahmed [now visibly upset]: 'Harry. Harry don't!'

Ahmed looks around and calls to his teacher: 'Cathy. Cathy' but Cathy has left the area and does not hear.

Ahmed catches Robert's eye: 'Harry bumped it. He bumped my bear.'

Robert [points out the bear mould]: 'Look – you can make another one.' He looks at Ahmed, who is still looking towards Cathy, who is at the other side of the playground. Robert then picks up the mould and presses it into the damp sand. 'Look Ahmed – I made another one.' Ahmed turns and looks at the new bear-castle and begins to dig again.

Robert [turns seriously to Harry and says, firmly]: 'This time, don't squash it.'

Conflicts between toddlers often revolve around the possession of objects, where individual wants win out over a consideration of the wants or property rights of the other. However, a desire to achieve dominance over one's peers has also been observed as a feature of toddlerhood (Licht, Simoni and Perrig-Chiello, 2008). While we cannot be sure of Harry's motivation, his action suggests a willing defiance of Ahmed's demand, and an apparent effort to exert power over the situation and elicit an effect from his peer. His actions appear consistent with Wittmer's (2008) description of conflicts as 'ego testing', during which young children explore questions such as 'What can I get away with?' and 'Who has the right?' (p. 102).

Conflicts can bring about the termination of social play. They can, though, also afford valuable opportunities to develop social understanding by providing children with first-hand experience of the ways in which one person's intentions may contrast with those of another, as well as the psychological effect that their actions have on their peers (Shin, 2012). Conflicts are therefore valuable opportunities to learn about other minds. Conflict situations also highlight the resilience of toddler relationships. Brownell and Kopp (2007) state that, when conflicts arise in play between 'fighting friends' (p. 181), these peers tend to find ways to resolve their conflict, enabling the play to continue. When this observation was shared with these children's educators and parents, words like *'problem-solver'*, *'peace-maker'* and *'mediator'* were used to describe the capable way in which Robert stepped in to resolve the disrupted play situation. Robert adopted the role of the 'pro-social' leader (Shin *et al.*, 2004), empathizing with Ahmed, finding a solution, and using direct words and actions to regulate Harry's future behaviour. Not only was Robert demonstrating an awareness of and sensitivity to his peers' emotions and intentions, but he was exercising leadership qualities of care, assertion and initiative to exert influence over the play and his peers.

A different perspective: the group within the culture

The final perspective to be considered in this chapter relates to the way in which the characteristics of children's peer relationships intersect with the features of their broader social and cultural world. The nature of relationships and interpersonal relatedness can be seen to be guided by pre-existing cultural structures and practices as children are motivated to engage in the kinds of social interactions and experiences that are valued, and therefore promoted by their community (Van Oers and Hännikäinen, 2001). Within a peer group context, culturally relevant activities have the potential to support close, reciprocal social interactions because the familiar, collectively known structure of the activity acts as a scaffold, allowing multiple children to participate cooperatively in group experiences (Degotardi and Pearson, 2010, and Chapter 4). Furthermore, collectively established values motivate children to engage in specific ways of relating to one another and to enter particular forms of relationship (Corsaro, 2012). By responding to and reproducing important experiences and ideas within the group context, children gain a sense of acceptance, as individuals who *belong* within the larger group context.

Peer group culture

Writing about the cultural nature of childhood and children's worlds, Corsaro (2012) states that 'Children produce and participate in their own unique peer cultures by creatively appropriating information from the adult world to address their own peer concerns' (p. 488). Although he argues that childhood, and the experiences it entails, are constrained by the social structures of a particular community, he uses the term *interpretive reproduction* to refer to the ways that children draw on their understanding of societal ways of being in order to create their own unique peer cultures.

The culture of the classroom

Corsaro (2012) explains that 'children are always participating in and are part of two cultures – their own and adults' – and these cultures are intricately inter-woven' (p. 489). This participation allows children to draw on their under-standing of existing cultural activities in which they participate, while contributing to the generation and regeneration of these experiences. The next observation exemplifies Corsaro's perspective on understanding the peer group within the culture.

It is late afternoon, and a small group of toddlers are listening to educator Kylie as she reads them a story. Once finished, Kylie moves away from the group, but Alistair imme-diately jumps up and fetches an animal picture book from the shelf. He slowly and delib-erately opens the first page, and his actions are noticed by Lucia, Annie and Ellen, who gather around and watch with interest. Alistair turns the pages slowly, and as he does so, he 'reads' the story as if he is anticipating the animal to appear on each page – 'It's a . . . Lion!' 'It's a . . . Snake!' Before long, the other children are joining in, watching with anticipation as Alistair turns the page and allowing him to say 'It's a . . .' before calling out the name of the revealed animal in unison. There is much laughter and excitement as each animal is revealed.

In this episode, we see Alistair drawing in the other children by taking the lead in an experience that is very familiar to himself and his peers. Locating this group experience within the larger culture, his educator, Min-Jee, explains: *'Children like to be like a teacher. I often see some children trying to read to other children.'* Similarly, teacher Cathy proposes that *'I suppose it's the imitation of what has just happened'*, but then goes on to note:

He's allowing the other children to take part. In the way he's asking them, 'What animal's this? What animal's that?' And he's allowing them to take the lead and then another one takes the lead. So, fair share.

Cathy recognizes that Alistair is taking a leadership role in this experience, but is doing so in a way that encourages peer participation. Corsaro (2000) argues that 'children make persistent attempts *to gain control* of their lives and to *share* that control with each other' (p. 92, original italics), and it would appear that this perspective is evident in Cathy's interpretation of the way in which Alistair has adapted the regular teacher-led classroom experience to create a cooperative activity in which he and his peers are all actively involved.

Experiences such as the one above demonstrate how children's participa-tion in routine or ritualized centre activities can involve relatedness at the community, as well as interpersonal, level. During such activities, children are following the rules and structures that have been established over time by participants in that particular setting, reflecting shared understandings of 'this is what *we* do' (Degotardi and Pearson, 2010). Gillespie (2006) draws on the thinking of George Herbert Mead, a contemporary of Dewey, to explain that it is during children's participation in these simple games that they first gain experience with communally shared roles and expectations. Engagement in childhood games, he argues, forms the basis of cooperative endeavours – of collective agency – and therefore establishes a sense of community and belonging. Mead describes children's motivation to engage in experiences by stating that 'it is a period in which he likes *to belong*' and goes on to explain that the child 'becomes something which can function in the organized whole, and thus tends to determine himself in his relationship with the group in which he belongs' (Mead, 1934, p. 160). What we see is the inseparable nature of social relationships and social context as 'such events are basic to producing and maintaining affiliative structure as well as cultural systems among the children' (Løkken, 2000, p. 172).

The culture of friendship

Friendship is regarded as one of the most important aspects of peer social relationships, with a large body of literature demonstrating that the ability to establish and maintain friendships has far-reaching social, emotional and cognitive developmental implications (Hay *et al.*, 2004; Howes, 2009). Most friendship studies, however, have explored the nature and implications of friendships for preschool and school-aged children, leading to a relative neglect of this type of relationship with infants and toddlers. The final topic to be addressed in this chapter is the question of whether very young children can indeed be considered as being and having friends.

In her book on children's friendships, Judy Dunn (2004) presents rich detail on the existence, characteristics and implications of children's friendships. She details how friendships can begin in toddlerhood, especially in contexts where children spend extended periods of time together. Howes (2008) states that young children's attendance in group-care contexts provides them with rich opportunities for the development of friendships. Drawing on three decades' work on infant–toddler social relatedness, she argues that:

> It is only within groups of peers that children develop both social interactions skills particular to peer interaction and construct social relationships particular to peers – friendships.
>
> (p. 553)

Howes goes on to explain that peer relationships are structured around a network of play partners that are readily available in group contexts. For this reason, early friendships can be regarded as an integral aspect of infant–toddler group culture, with observational studies demonstrating that particular children seek out, and want to play with, selected familiar peers (Whaley and Rubenstein, 1994; Howes, 1996; Engdahl, 2012). In our study, certain children were observed and described by educators and parents to have definite play partner preferences. Harry, Robert and Ahmed, for example, were rarely apart during their time at the centre, and their preference for one another featured strongly in the interview data with parents:

He always talks about Robert [Ahmed's mum].
Now he does talk a fair bit about Harry . . . 'I played with Harry today' [Robert's mum].

Furthermore, peer group stability allows friendships to form and be maintained, as young children draw on a shared history of experiences and interactions to strengthen their knowledge of and commitment towards one another (Howes, 2009). As Robert's mum explained:

I guess just having this common thread that they've had since . . . they've been together since the baby room . . . I think it's just sharing those experiences together and they can relate to each other . . . they've known each other for nearly a year.

Friendships are also characterized by mutual affection, support and companionship, all of which have featured in many of the data episodes presented in this chapter. Robert's attempt to find a solution for the conflict between Harry and Ahmed is a clear example of a willingness to provide emotional support for his peer. Holly's offering of the feather to Ahmed was interpreted by Holly's mother in the context of a recognized friendship relationship:

I think it shows that she wanted to show Ahmed that she still cares about him, so he wouldn't get upset that she rejected him.

The children in this study therefore frequently engaged in behaviours that reflected attempts to 'do friendship' (Engdahl, 2012). Friendship, though, was more than a feature of the group-care context; the efforts and comments of the educators, parents and the children demonstrated that it was a highly valued component of the cultural life at the centre. Children did not only 'do friendship', but they discussed and defined it as well:

It is lunchtime and 2-year-old Kim, 20-month-old Annie and 28-month-old Robert are sitting next to one another at the table. After some general chatter about the chicken and vegetable meal that has been served, Annie turns to Kim:

Annie: I like chicken. Do you like chicken?

Kim [responds]: I like chicken. Do you like chicken?

Annie: Yes. I like chicken . . . [pause] . . . are you my friend?

Kim: Yes. I am your friend.

Annie [turns to Robert]: Do you like chicken?

Robert: Yes.

Annie: Are you my friend?

Kim: Are you my friend Robert?

Robert: Yes.

De Haan and Singer (2001) note how friendship was explicitly labelled and discussed during their observations of the play interactions of 3- to 5-year-old children. While older children tended to use such labels in a conditional manner (for example, 'you're not my friend'), younger ones used it to express affiliation with the group. Singer and De Haan explain how young children's friendships are often formed around the establishment of values and likes, and the interaction between Annie, Kim and Robert seems to indicate the beginning of this process, with these very young children apparently associating shared likes with friendship. Educator, Min-Jee explained, '*It's like we have things in common*', and Cathy added:

They are quite close – they want to do the same things and they want to . . . 'if you like this, I'll like this' and 'you like that, I'll like that'.

The presence of similarity and familiarity therefore features strongly in toddler friendships, supporting affiliations between individual children, and contributing towards a sense of belonging to, and membership in, the larger group.

Some final thoughts

The excerpts presented in this chapter illustrate, without doubt, the important fact that infant–toddler peer relationships shape their experiences in infant–toddler early education and care settings. We have seen how peer relationships among very young children show all the characteristics of relationship dimensions and functions outlined in Chapter 3, and the data presented demonstrate the impressive social capabilities that these young children can bring to their peer group contexts. It is certainly clear that infants and toddlers are, in no way, the solitary, egocentric learners that they were thought to be in the past.

Like most human beings, infants and toddlers not only construct relationships, they also derive significant learning benefits from the process of being 'filled with a variety of actions and expectations from their various relationships' with peers (Auhagen and von Salisch, 1996, p. 1). By focusing on peer-group processes, we therefore not only develop understandings of the purpose of particular forms of relatedness for individual children's learning and development, but can also see how shared experiences and meanings are collaboratively constructed by groups of peers, and the significance of these shared experiences for the lived reality in the infant–toddler classroom.

7 Realizing the potential of relationship-based pedagogies

Children need adults who work with their eyes and minds wide open – ready themselves to learn, to think, to reflect.

Jools Page, Ann Clare and Cathy Nutbrown

Throughout this book, we have portrayed early childhood centres as relationship-rich places that comprise many different types of relationship, all of which can contribute towards the learning, development and wellbeing of infants, their families and educators. In Chapter 1, we framed our endeavour with reference to wide international support for relationship-based approaches to be integrated into the early childhood curriculum and pedagogy. In subsequent chapters, we provided theoretical, research- and practice-based evidence to describe the multitude of ways in which relationships are viewed, formed and enacted in infant–toddler classrooms.

In this final chapter we come full circle, revisiting the notion of relationship-based pedagogy and drawing together key themes that have been apparent throughout the presentation, discussion and interpretation of our research data. We use the above quote by Page, Clare and Nutbrown (2013, p. 9) as both a starting and a finishing point. Advocating for the need for high-quality infant–toddler professional practice, Page and colleagues stress the need to think carefully about issues of quality in infant–toddler programmes. They emphasize the importance of well-qualified educators who have a thorough knowledge of infant–toddler learning, development and all of the processes that come into play when working closely with these young children and their families. Most importantly, though, they argue that:

> Children need to spend their days with people who 'think outside the box'. They need to spend time with adults who ask 'why' – who know why they do what they do. Adults who can articulate their pedagogy make the best practitioners – for they can open themselves to

> self-scrutiny and reflect on the processes they have been involved in
> with the children.
>
> (p. 9)

Sound, thoughtful and intentional decision-making is the basis of professional practice, and this ability is reliant on a willingness to learn and reflect critically on knowledge bases, concepts and viewpoints. Through opportunities to engage with, discuss and think about different ideas and perspectives, educators come to see more clearly the value of what they do. This deeper understanding flows into their professional work with young children, families, colleagues and communities, and therefore has the potential to enhance professionalism within the early childhood sector, and raise the status and self-efficacy of those working with our youngest children.

We therefore use our final words to consider the value of relationship-based approaches to learning and teaching for all involved, as well as issues that need to be considered in the endeavour to create and implement a rich relationship-based approach to teaching and learning with infants and toddlers.

Why do we need relationship-based approaches to infant–toddler programmes?

Relationship-based pedagogies have, at their core, a commitment to building, strengthening and maintaining relationships between children, their educators and community members. But why is this important? Throughout this book, we have illustrated the value of working closely and collaboratively with young children, their parents and other professionals. In this section, we draw these threads together to discuss two over-arching benefits of relationship-based approaches for those who are directly involved in infant–toddler programmes.

Being and belonging

At the heart of early childhood programmes lies a desire to contribute positively towards the lives of those who participate in those programmes (Shonkoff, 2006). While a need to foster long-term development and wellbeing is central to this aim, relationship-based approaches require us to think beyond the notion of 'becoming' to also consider individuals' present and lived experiences in the classroom. What does it mean to *be* an individual in this context, and how does this contribute towards a sense of a belonging within the extended group of children, their families and educators?

Throughout the course of this book, we have seen examples of how self-identity and self-worth are constructed through the ways that individuals relate to others and others relate to them. We have seen children receive assistance, affection and feedback from their peers; care, attention and responsiveness from their educators; and have read about the benefits of educators and parents respecting one another's experiences and contributions to the lives of young children. All of these actions and more go further than creating feelings of 'suitability' in the early childhood centre (Brooker, 2009). As Woodhead and Brooker (2008) explain:

> Belonging is the relational dimension of personal identity, the funda-
> mental psycho-social 'glue' that locates every individual (babies,
> children and adults) at a particular position in space, time and human
> society and – most important – connects people to each other.
>
> (p. 3)

This conceptualization of belonging, according to Sumsion and Wong (2011), reflects 'the allure of a relational and collective endeavor that speaks, almost seductively, to a deep-seated desire for connectedness' (p. 37). By building and strengthening relationships, it is possible to create communities in which all stakeholders experience social and emotional connections to others in the programme. Such connections are critical channels for the development and support of emotional wellbeing and self-identity, both of which are central to present and future human functioning.

The implications of relationship-based approaches extend beyond the establishment of social and emotional connections. As we have seen, the very processes of relating depend on opportunities to interact with others; to discuss, negotiate and work together to establish shared experiences and interactions (Meeuwig, 2008). This itself is underpinned by a willingness to acknowledge, respect and respond to the points of view of others, their feelings, needs, goals and aspirations, and ideas. Relationship-based pedagogies are therefore reliant on opportunities for, and openness to, the kinds of inter-actions that allow each individual to actively participate in the education and care programme. The concept of belonging sits well with those who advocate for an incorporation of the United Nations Conventions on the Rights of the Child (1989) into early childhood programmes (Woodhead and Brooker, 2008). As explained in Chapter 5, agency and citizenship are promoted when children are allowed to contribute towards their own learning and lived experiences in meaningful ways (Corsaro, 2005; Berthelsen, Brownlee and Johansson, 2009), and this can be done only when children's capabilities are recognized, and their perspectives are expressed, heard and taken seriously. When this opportunity is extended to families and educators, classrooms become a site for ethical, democratic practice (Moss, 2007), where all are empowered to participate fully and contribute to the programme. By putting into place measures that can foster the development of mutually responsive relationships, all involved can play a part in the creation of belonging within the classroom.

Teaching and learning

The second reason to advocate a commitment to relationship-based approaches is a pedagogical one. Early childhood professional literature pays tribute to the idea of 'teaching and learning *through* relationships'; an idea summed up by Brooker (2007), as follows:

> Learning is now seen to be very much the outcome of relationships: between children and their friends and classmates, between children and the adults who care for them in every setting, and between the professional educators and the families and communities who have provided children's earliest experiences.
>
> (p. 14)

If learning is an outcome of relationships, how does this learning actually transpire? An answer to this question can be found in the theoretical proposition that learning and development are socially and collaboratively constructed. For some time, early childhood thinking has drawn on Vygotsky's zone of proximal development (Vygotsky, 1978), Bruner's principle of scaffolding (Wood, Bruner and Ross, 1976) and Rogoff's concepts of guided participation (Rogoff, 1998) to conceptualize how learning can be facilitated during social interactions. In recent times, these theoretical ideas have been developed to include the concept of *sustained shared thinking*, which is increasingly regarded as a feature of effective early childhood teaching. Sustained shared thinking is defined by Siraj-Blatchford and colleagues (2008) as 'an effective pedagogical process that involves an adult being aware of the child's interest and understandings and involves the adult and child interacting together to develop an idea or skill' (p. 29). Meaningful interactions are at the heart of this process – in particular, interactions in which ideas are expressed, explored and expanded in a sustained and collaborative manner.

Accordingly, learning and teaching *through* relationships is reliant on dialogue that involves 'reciprocal and multivoiced exchanges of ideas that direct the path of learning' (Papatheodorou, 2009, p. 10). These exchanges comprise more than simply what is said and done, to include a 'space between' individuals within which perspectives are expressed and inferences made: 'What are your intentions?', 'How do you feel?', 'What are your interests?', 'What do you know?' and 'What do you think?' Answers to these questions provide educators with working hypotheses that allow them to adapt their teaching strategies and learning provisions to suit the understandings, learning styles and interests of individuals and groups of children (Bruner, 1996). They enable children to establish interactions with their peers where they draw on shared knowledge and motivations to create experiences that support and enhance one another's learning. And they pave the way for educators and parents to engage in the kinds of respectful conversation through which they can learn more about one another and the children in their care, and which assists endeavours to work together for the benefit of children's learning. Relationship-based pedagogies therefore involve the collaborative and interactive construction of new knowledge and understandings through the reciprocal expression and interpretation of perspectives (Van Oers and Hännikäinen, 2001). Children, educators and family members are all members of a community of minds (Nelson, 2007) in which individual and shared perspectives contribute significantly towards the process of learning.

Issues to consider

For these reasons, it is evident that there are substantial merits associated with relationship-based approaches to curriculum and pedagogy in infant–toddler programmes. Throughout this book we have presented an account of the complexity, intricacies and diversities related to infants' and toddlers' relationship worlds. From our discussion and analysis, two points have become increasingly clear:

1 there is no single or preferred relationship-based approach, as relationships and perspectives about relationships will vary between individuals, groups, centres and cultures
2 there is no single formula for developing and implementing a relationship-based approach, as relationship priorities will be context-specific, based on the theoretical and practice-based viewpoints associated with any given setting.

While a single approach is both unachievable and undesirable, there are some key issues that are common across many of the relationship perspectives we have addressed in this book. The importance of these issues becomes evident once one recognizes a major challenge associated with relationship-based approaches to learning and teaching. We have argued throughout that interactions lie at the core of relationships and of relationship-based approaches. It is through interactions that relationships are able to be built and sustained, and the dynamics of these interactions will both enable and constrain the kinds of learning opportunities that relationships afford (Weiss, 1974; Hinde, 1997; Lewis, 2005). *Yet* research has told us that interactions between educators and parents can be fraught with tensions resulting from clashing expectations and roles (e.g. Hohmann, 2007). Less than optimal working conditions, including perceptions of low status, isolation, poor access to professional support and learning opportunities, and high staff turnover are barriers to staff collegiality and cooperation (Goouch and Powell, 2013). Interactions between educators and infants and toddlers have been reported to focus on regulating behaviours, directing attention and preventing conflicts, rather than on the rich, reciprocal interactions reported in Chapter 5 (e.g. Smith, 1999; Durden and Dangel, 2008; Davis and Degotardi, in press). Finally, the pervasive view of the solitary, egocentric, exploratory infant can limit opportunities afforded to these very young children to interact with their peers (Degotardi and Pearson, 2010; McGaha *et al.*, 2012).

It would seem, therefore, that there are many barriers that can prevent the kinds of interactions that support relationship development and relationship-based pedagogies in infant–toddler settings. Yet in this book, we have presented research data to illustrate that these barriers can be overcome, enabling relationships to be built, and learning and development potentials to be realized. So what are some issues that need to be considered by those wanting to develop and strengthen relationship-based approaches? In the next section, we examine issues of 'time', 'space', 'place', 'hearts' and 'minds', with an aim of identifying key implications for those working towards maximizing relationship opportunities within their infant–toddler programmes.

Time

In Chapter 1, we challenged the idea that relationships are formed easily, explaining that relationships are not formed via an instant, magnetic attraction, but instead take time and effort to develop and sustain. As we saw in Chapter 4, time is a crucial factor at periods of transition. It takes time for individuals to make adjustments to new people and places, to become comfortable with one another, and to know one another in terms of interaction styles, needs, interests and expectations. Relationships, though, not only *take* time, they also call for an *investment* in time. We explained how this investment permits authentic interactions to take place, as each individual gains trust in, and opens up to, the other. Such processes cannot be rushed, so an investment in time, especially at periods of transition and relationship realignment will reap benefits in terms of how relationships are formed and the kinds of relationships that result.

Time is also a factor when we remember that relationships are founded and maintained on the basis of shared histories of interactions and experiences. When individuals meet regularly and engage in similar activities, they build a shared repertoire of scripts and interaction styles that support interpersonal relatedness. By permitting the establishment of a shared knowledge base about 'what we can do' and 'how we can be' with others in the group, *time together* provides the context for the enactment of present and future relationships. This highlights the significance of the organizational attendance structures that are implemented in any infant–toddler programme. While attendance in these education and care settings is increasing, part-time enrolment is common, with many children attending at different times of the week and across different parts of the day. A consequence of these comings and goings can be that many infants and toddlers have restricted opportunities to spend regular time periods together. When paired with fluctuating staff work shifts, the resulting discontinuity in regular contacts can mean that young children, their parents and educators have limited time to get to know one another at any more than a superficial level (De Groot Kim, 2010).

A series of studies in the United States by Recchia and colleagues highlights other important ways that time is implicated in relationship-based approaches. In one study, Recchia (2012) explores aspects of continuity and discontinuity in two young children's and their educators' experiences as the toddlers transitioned into the infant room and then moved on to the preschool room. When the children transitioned to the older children's room, a major challenge reported by the preschool educators related to these young children's ability to undertake tasks on cue, with educators expecting that older toddlers will easily and quickly adapt to new expectations and routines. When this did not occur with one child, staff expressed frustration and reported that it was more difficult to form a close relationship with that child. Time was implicated in two ways in the children's reaction to their transition:

1   A lack of continuity in expectations and structure across the transition period was a significant factor. The preschool room schedule was reported to be relatively rigid, with the children expected to adjust to the time structures of the room. In contrast, the infant room had more fluid time structures, which responded to each individual child's routine.

2   In the infant room, educators reported that they allowed children extended periods of time to pursue their current interests and concerns, and that their willingness to follow the infants' lead contributed to the development and consolidation of their relationships. In contrast, the preschool teachers focused on helping the children join the larger group structures. When one of the toddlers resisted this move, the educators reported that the resulting conflict established a distance that ultimately impacted negatively on their relationship with that child.

From this research, we can identify that time is a factor, both in terms of the patterns of expectations and interactions that are built up between the young child and his/her educators, and the willingness of educators to be flexible in terms of their provision of time to the child. This provision, in the form of a slower, more relaxed pace of interactions, allows the kind of sustained, give-and-take responsive interactions that support relationship-based learning and teaching, as well as the development of close, mutually responsive and respectful relationships. Infants are given the time they need to adjust to new situations and participate in learning experiences at their own pace, and a relaxed pace reduces infant and educator stress, maximizing opportunities for each individual to be socially and emotionally open to and accepting of the other (Recchia and Dvorakova, 2012). Educators are allowed to '*take their time*' to closely observe infants' preferences and learning styles, and are thus able to respond in an individualized and attuned manner. In a study of infant–educator interactions, Recchia and Shin (2012) found this affordance allowed infant educators to get to know their children deeply, and adapt their responses to accommodate individual capabilities and styles:

> When infant teachers were able to realize the infants' specific intentions, read their cues accurately, and respond to each infant appropriately, infants and teachers were able to share meaningful joint understanding and successful social interactions and thus be in synch within the infant rooms.
>
> (p. 1559)

It is through these close, synchronized interactions that group cultures, comprising shared meanings and practices, can be collectively constructed.

Time also brings about change. In many ways, relationships are moving targets, with the growth and development of each individual meaning that the nature of the relationship between them will constantly evolve. It is because relationships are so dynamic that the ability to perceive and adapt to changing capabilities, needs, expectations and priorities of the other over time is important. The result is that interpersonal relatedness is in a constant flux of being in *and* out of synch. This applies to relationships between adults and between infant–toddler peers as much as it does to infant/toddler-educator interactions, where the ever-changing and subjective nature of human relatedness means that complete synchrony is as elusive as it is attractive. Even in the closest of relationships, there is always an element of difference, of discordance brought about by different ideas, opinions and interests. However, episodes of 'out-of-synch' interactions provide opportunities for relationship development. They provide the impetus to both educators and young children to express their perspectives in order to clarify their feelings, intentions and ideas. When time is taken, given and invested in all aspects of social interactions, multiple opportunities are created for the engagement in meaningful dialogue, and for the learning, teaching and community-building benefits that these dialogues can afford.

Space

Although relationships certainly need and are affected by time, they also require space to develop and thrive. Throughout the chapters, we have presented data showing the significance of interacting, playing and working together. We noted how children sought and maintained physical closeness with one another and with their educators, both at play and during other routine or transition times. In the context of relationships between educators and parents, we outlined the importance of having opportunities to have meaningful, professional conversations during which information and ideas can be shared and discussed. All of these experiences would not happen without the provision of space, as it is space that provides the locations in which meetings can occur, interactions can take place and communities can be formed.

In our introductory chapter we recognized that formal infant–toddler education and care programmes constitute unique spaces for development and learning. As institutional contexts, infant–toddler rooms are usually purposefully designed with groups of children and adults in mind. As learning spaces, furnishing and materials are provided and organized in order to permit certain types of experience to take place. For these reasons, infant–toddler rooms, and the spaces that they contain, are never neutral, but are instead reflections of the values, priorities, philosophies and understandings of those who inhabit that space (Curtis and Carter, 2003). While it is tempting to think about space as simply involving room arrangement, there are other issues that need to be addressed if we wish to consider how space is implicated in the creation and maintenance of relationships within any particular infant–toddler setting.

From Finland, Niina Rutanen's research on toddler environments provides a more detailed way of conceptualizing the production of space (Rutanen, 2012; Rutanen, 2014). Rutanen draws on Henry Lefebvre's work on social space to explore the organization of space, in terms of the priorities and social practices of both educators and the children. At the broadest level, the organization of space is a product of culturally constructed meanings, which, in this context, reflects cultural and institutional ideologies about what is best for young children, their families and educators. These ideologies result in the provision and organization of spaces for defined purposes. For example, in Chapter 5 we detailed how the value of parent–educator partnerships is espoused in early childhood curriculum documents in a number of countries. This policy direction may encourage centres to create spaces where educators and parents can meet, communicate with one another, and forge the kinds of relationship that are enshrined in policy to indicate quality in early childhood programmes. Similarly, in our own research, the strong emphasis by parents and educators on the care aspect of educator–infant relationships may well have been reflected in the provision of defined spaces within the classroom for joint educator–infant play, and the positioning of educators and children during one-on-one and small-group interactions.

Space can also be defined at a much more local level, through the lived experiences of those who inhabit that space. Rutanen (2012) argues that some spaces are flexible, and are organized and restructured by educators' and children's personal experiences and interpersonal relationships. In this way, space is not *provided*, but is instead *appropriated* for personal or collective benefit. In Rutanen's study, educators reported arranging space to provide opportunities for active play and to establish some control over what children could and could not play with, and to promote certain types of social interaction between the children. Davis and Degotardi (in press) also detail how Australian educators' organization of materials in the space can influence social relatedness, with educators reporting that plenty of toys are needed in order to minimize the occurrence of conflicts over possessions. Together, these examples demonstrate how the organization of space often reflects a tension between a desire to allow active social physical engagement and a need to moderate potential risks (Hännikäinen and Rutanen, 2013).

While adults are undeniably powerful when it comes to the management of space, the children in our research demonstrated how they themselves actively engage with space within their programmes. When examining the complexity of togetherness in peer relationships, we saw how children used and structured their classroom space to enable their engagement in gleeful, physical and humourous games (see also Løkken, 2000). Rutanen (2014) explains that children are particularly capable at defining space when claiming or protecting their territory. When discussing cooperation and negotiation, we presented data to illustrate how toddlers guarded and debated boundaries of personal space, and how they could competently resolve conflicts that resulted from breaches of this space.

Curtis and Carter (2003) describe how early childhood education has a long and rich history that stresses the instructive power of space, and in doing so, call on educators to 'reexamine every inch of our environments for the messages they convey' (p. 4). Space, we have seen, is a dynamic and value-laden construct that, when used thoughtfully, acts so as to promote and constrain different types of social relationship across educators, parents and children. When seen as a flexible provision, space also reflects social agency and permits active participation, control and decision-making within the classroom. In both cases, space is a socially constructed and significant educator that assumes a central role in the relationship climate of the classroom.

Place

A third significant theme that is apparent across the course of this book is that interpersonal relationships are best understood with reference to the culture in which individuals and groups reside. Context-bound norms and practices support and constrain the opportunities for relationship formation, and will influence the ways that individual relationships are played out within any particular cultural setting (Mamali, 1996; Duck, 1999). We have seen, for example, how particular childhood games, songs and classroom activities comprise expressions of classroom and family culture that, because they are known by multiple members of the group, form the basis for shared and collaborative experiences. In our research sites, we also saw how particular relationship functions, such as friendship and affection, are actively supported as they are regarded by parents, educators and children as desirable features of peer culture.

The beliefs and expectations of any social or cultural group therefore influence the kinds of relationship that are promoted in any given setting, and discourage forms of relatedness that contradict these value systems (Super and Harkness, 1986; Kâğıtçıbaşı, 2007). For this reason, in Chapter 1 we acknowledged the cultural situatedness of the ideas and research data presented in our book. While we have drawn on international research to discuss and interpret our own data and ideas, it is apparent that the vast majority of this research is drawn from Australasian, European or Anglo-American contexts. Although this reflects the current state of play in infant–toddler education and care professional and research literature, it should not lull us into assuming that the views or practices expressed in this book can be universally generalized.

There is, in fact, emerging evidence to suggest that important differences occur in relationships perspectives both within and between cultures. Rockel (2005), for example, examines the practice of primary caregiving, popular in both New Zealand and the United Kingdom, which is based on the premise that infants benefit most when cared for by one consistent educator. While she acknowledges that this practice may support the establishment of secure attachments, she questions whether it is appropriate in Maori early childhood centres, where care is traditionally provided by multiple caregivers and peers. In Finland (Hännikäinen and Rutanen, 2013) a study of early childhood university lecturers' and researchers' opinions about the most important theoretical perspectives to inform infant–toddler pedagogy found that responses often ran counter to attachment theory ideas relating to the primacy of one secure educator–infant relationship and, instead, drew on notions of togetherness, intentionality and social-communication to underline infants' capacity to form multiple relationships with educators, peers and family members. Hujala and colleagues (2009) also report cultural variation in educators' views about the desired attributes of educator–parent relationships across five European countries. While educators in Norway, Estonia, Lithuania and Portugal attributed an active role to parents in terms of their contribution to the activities of the early childhood centre, Finnish educators attributed a much more passive role. Educators from the Baltic countries were more likely than those in the other countries to emphasize their role in advising parents on child-rearing practices. The researchers suggest that the relative status of early childhood educators across these different countries may result in varying levels of differentiation between the parenting and professional role, which ultimately affects the desired dynamics of educator–parent relationships within that country.

The picture that is emerging from this research is that global diversity exists in relationship perspectives and characteristics. It highlights the need for more international research to be conducted, especially in non-European or non-Western cultures, where data about infant–toddler education and care programmes remains, to date, largely unknown to the English-speaking world (for some recent contributions in non-Western contexts, see Lee and Jessee, 1997; Newport, 2000; Kim and Moon, 2011). Knowledge of a range of cultural and context-specific perspectives will not only broaden the knowledge base in regards to the existence of variations between countries, but will also help to address the reality of the broad cultural diversity that exists in contemporary society within many countries. It prompts those who design and implement relationship-based programmes to actively engage with multiple perspectives at both global and local levels to ensure the relevance of their approaches for all children, families and educators.

Hearts

During the course of this book, we have discussed how relationships often involve and evoke strong expressions of emotions. Existing emotional ties and bonds are stretched as infants, toddlers and their families transition into the infant–toddler classroom, with processes of separation and new relationships formation often 'tugging the heart strings' of all involved. As discussed in Chapters 3 and 4, emotions also come into play, in the form of trust and security between relationships partners which, on the one hand, bring about feelings of ease and comfort and, on the other, stir up feelings of discomfort, distress and anxiety. In Chapter 5, we discussed concepts of care and love to propose that caring for others involves a strong, empathetic commitment towards supporting others' emotional experiences and needs. When exploring peer relationships we saw how relationships can bring about a strong sense of emotional satisfaction as well as frustration and displeasure. Therefore, while it is appealing to associate interpersonal relationships with positive emotions, reality shows that strong and close relationships will also involve conflicts and personal stress. It is evident that, across all relationship types and contexts, we can expect that a full range of positive and negative emotions will be expressed and experienced by all stakeholders in the programme.

To be effective in their professional role, infant–toddler educators therefore need to be accepting of, and able to work with, strong feelings and expressions of emotions. In their work with baby-room practitioners in the United Kingdom, Goouch and Powell (2013) found that infant educators cited emotional resilience as being an essential characteristic of those who work effectively with this young age group. The practitioners in this project described their work as emotional labour, involving relentless pressures to meet the often fragile and demanding needs of infants and their families. Rockel and Craw (2011) identify a romanticized quest for happiness as a source of stress, claiming that educators strongly feel a need to ensure that all involved in the infant–toddler setting – infants, parents and staff – are happy. Not only is infant happiness seen as a driving force behind curriculum and pedagogical choices in the setting, but also parents' and managements' perceptions of happiness can have a major impact on feelings of self-efficacy:

> The parent may desire 'a contented child' for reassurance that the place is contributing to their security; for the teacher an (un)happy child might reflect on whether or not they are seen as a 'good teacher'; and the early childhood centre employer wishes for the performance of 'happy workers' for a successful business.
>
> (p. 128)

The work of Peter Elfer (2007, 2012) and Julia Manning-Morton (2006) has contributed to an increased understanding of the emotional pressures of infant–toddler professional practice. Their research supports that of Goouch and Powell, showing that practitioners often feel compelled to try to maintain a harmonious working climate by eliciting positive emotional responses from infants and their parents. They also acknowledge the psychological complexity of having to deal regularly with the intensity of their own and others' negative emotions, explaining that the pressure to act and react calmly and professionally in the face of emotionally difficult situations requires teachers to regulate their own emotions. Negative feelings can also come in the form of tiredness and discomfort related to the physical aspect of the work (Manning-Morton, 2006). Such challenges can prove detrimental to the relationships that are formed and played out in the infant–toddler room as they can cause educators to 'shut off' emotionally and communicatively, preventing them from connecting with young children and their parents in authentic and empathetic ways.

Another kind of emotional labour can present itself in the form of internal or managerial conflicts about how emotionally involved or attached educators should become with infants, toddlers and their families. Elfer (2007) argues that while, on one hand, educators understand the significance of supportive and secure relationships, they often feel obliged to maintain a professional distance in the name of protecting the parent–child relationship and protecting themselves from emotional upset when they, or the family, move on. As the process of forming and sustaining any relationship requires a commitment to, and investment in, that relationship (Hinde, 1997; Duck, 1999), it is clear how such internal conflicts would constrain the quality of relationships that the teacher is able to form with the children and their families.

The emotional labour of early childhood work is often overlooked or undervalued, so both Elfer (2007, 2012) and Manning-Morton (2006) argue that there is a need to establish provisions to allow educators to actively engage with the emotional aspect of their work, thus enabling feelings to be acknowledged and validated. In Chapter 5, we discussed how professional growth has strong implications for the ways in which professionals can work cooperatively and collegially. Having opportunities to discuss and come to terms with emotional demands can promote teacher wellbeing by boosting emotional resilience. Allowing educators to critically reflect on the emotional aspect of their work also fosters emotional intelligence in the form of a greater understanding of their own and others' emotional perspectives, and the relationship between personal reactions and professional practice. If, as we have argued throughout, issues of the heart are important features of relationships, the emotional aspect of infant–toddler practice needs to be acknowledged and addressed if educators are to approach emotionally demanding situations with an open and accepting mind.

Minds

The concluding statement above brings us to our final issue. We introduced this book by defining relationships as complex constructs that involve both behavioural and psychological components. Drawing on Hinde's seminal work, we explained how the nature of any one relationship is influenced by the minds, or perspectives, of the individuals involved. In this book we have sought to highlight just how important these thoughts, opinions and motivations are. In Chapter 3, we explored how parents and teachers focused on different aspects of two young children's relationships when explaining what they saw as significant characteristics of their interactions. In Chapter 4, we described how important it is for educators to develop an awareness of the priorities and concerns of parents and infants as they forge new relationships with one another within the classroom. The importance of negotiation and establishing shared understandings was discussed in Chapter 5, both in the context of parent–educator relationships as well as in the acknowledgement and encouragement of agency during educator–infant interactions. Finally, in Chapter 6, when we explored the nature of peer relationships, we saw how children's own developing understanding of others' needs, intentions and ideas can contribute to the development of togetherness, cooperation and peer culture.

The capacity and willingness to engage with these psychological aspects is therefore fundamental to relationship-based approaches to infant–toddler education and care. In Australia, Brownlee and Berthelsen's work on *personal epistemology* has investigated this professional attribute in infant–toddler educators (2006). Personal epistemology is a form of metacognition ('thinking about thinking') that refers to individual beliefs about the acquisition and subjective nature of knowledge. Epistemological beliefs can range from 'dualistic', where knowledge is regarded as being absolute and factual, to 'relativistic', where knowledge is seen as subjective and open to change. Brownlee and Berthelsen found that educators' epistemological beliefs had implications for their teaching across a range of contexts, as follows.

- Infant–toddler educators who held relativistic beliefs were likely to adhere to the importance of allowing infants and toddlers to construct their own knowledge through processes of inquiry, problem solving and decision-making. In contrast, those with less sophisticated, dualistic beliefs tended to focus on behaviour reproduction through modelling and observation (Brownlee, Berthelsen and Boulton-Lewis, 2004).
- Educators and student teachers who held relativistic beliefs were more open to self-reflection and possibilities of change than their dualistic colleagues, and were also more likely to be able to reflect deeply on processes of their own learning, change and professional development (Brownlee, 2001; Berthelsen, Brownlee and Boulton-Lewis, 2002).

Consistent with the themes underpinning this book, Brownlee, Berthelsen and colleagues argue that the professional insight associated with sophisticated epistemological beliefs is at the heart of relational pedagogy, as it allows educators to make connections between personal, practical and theoretical perspectives in order to facilitate their own and others' learning.

Another form of metacognition to receive recent attention is that of *mind-mindedness*. Originally coined in a parenting context by Elizabeth Meins (in Meins *et al.*, 1998), mind-mindedness involves being willing and able to 'get inside' a young child's head – to consider the child's perspective or way of understanding the world, rather than simply attending to physical needs and behaviours. In the context of early childhood education, this process comes into play through the concept of 'image of the child' as a psychological being, and represents a tendency to interpret young children's observable behaviour in terms of their intentions, feelings and thoughts.

In Chapter 5, we described how the *Understanding Infants* study explored the nature and complexity of educators' narrative interpretations of observed infant behaviours. In a follow-up to this analysis, we also investigated the extent to which mind-mindedness was demonstrated in these narrated interpretations (Degotardi and Sweller, 2012). We found that some practitioners focused heavily on describing observed behaviours, such as '*He's making sounds – normally whenever he takes two things together, he'll bang them together.*' In contrast, other interpretations were more mind-minded, interpreting the observed behaviours in light of the infants' mental states and processes:

she's, um, interested in what she's doing and is focused on it and will glance at what I'm doing but . . . if she doesn't want to do it then she won't do it – this is how she's strong-willed . . . it must be quite fascinating for her to see something that looks so different to what she's used to.

We were interested in the implications of these different levels of mind-mindedness for infant–educator interactions and relatedness, and our results showed that practitioners whose interpretations were more mind-minded were rated as being more sensitive and stimulating during their play interactions with that infant than those who tended towards more behavioural interpretations. In their actions, 'mind-minded' educators appeared 'in synch' with the infants, demonstrating a level of attunement to infants' perceptual, emotional and intellectual states that was less apparent with less 'mind-minded' educators. Our research found that levels of mind-mindedness in educators' interpretations *about* infants were also significantly related to the number of mind-related words they used when talking *to* these infants during play. In Chapter 5, we explained how words like 'want', 'try', 'think' and 'know' bring individual perspectives out into the open to be shared and negotiated during social interactions. Exposure to mind-related talk has implications for infants' developing understanding of their own and other mental states, which in turn, has been shown to be associated with children's ability to play and interact in connected and collaborative ways (Brownell *et al.*, 2006). It also has implications for the collaborative construction of learning, which, according to van Oers and Hännikäinen (2001), 'requires reflection on one's own understandings and comparing understandings among participants in a discourse' (p. 105). From this perspective, learning can be seen to be a relational process as teachers and children co-construct understandings through the exchange of thoughts and ideas within the context of meaningful social activity.

Moving forward: living and learning together

What we call the beginning is often the end. And to make an end is to make a beginning. The end is where we start from.

T.S. Eliot (1942)

Throughout this book we have focused on three interrelated messages. The first is that infants' relationship worlds are complex, comprising multiple relationships that have both common and unique characteristics depending on context and relationship type. Because of (and despite) this complexity, we have argued that, by understanding the diverse features and functions of the many relationships at play in infant–toddler early childhood programmes, it is possible to create opportunities to strengthen these relationships and enhance the learning opportunities that relationships provide. When acting as 'thoughtful agents', educators seek to increase their knowledge about those with whom they have relationships, about the nature and potential of these relationships, and about their own teaching practice.

The second message is that professional understandings can be enriched through the consideration of multiple perspectives from both theory and practice. An awareness of multiple perspectives increases the number of ways that any given event can be interpreted, thereby enabling educators' appreciation of the significance and potential of that event for all involved. By presenting and interpreting relationship research data from a range of theoretical perspectives, we argue that 'listening to' and 'dialoging' with different perspectives is integral to a relationship-based approach. Each perspective provides an additional lens through which educators can understand what they see and experience, and through which informed and thoughtful teaching practice can be framed. It allows us to focus on different aspects of the relationship story: individual, dyadic and cultural processes can be explored and explained, ultimately allowing educators to develop a richer knowledge base from which to launch their efforts to enhance different kinds and features of relationships.

Finally, we have argued that an engagement with multiple perspectives opens possibilities for change. By being open to, and considering, various theoretical lenses and points of view, educators have a well-stocked professional 'toolkit' with which to approach the diversity and dynamics of infant–toddler relationships. Multiple perspectives challenge educators to see things differently, to consider alternatives and reflect on their own ideas and practices, a process that is vital if we are to take seriously the call to acknowledge and incorporate diversity in the early childhood field. Moss (2010) argues that early childhood education contains a myriad of approaches – both theoretical and practice based – which, if ignored, runs the risk of advancing the kinds of normalized and decontextualized practice that disregards diversity and complexity. He calls on educators to embrace the need to 'think in context' as well as 'think the complex' and, in doing so, recognize that they, and all others in the early childhood community, have generalized and localized understandings and perspectives to offer in any given situation. Conflict between perspectives is inevitable, but it is also a necessity if we value the democratic participation of all involved. Yet, as Vandenbroeck (2009) states, a consideration of multiple perspectives necessitates

> time and space to allow ourselves to ask the difficult questions about how the dispute compels us to rethink our conceptions of what 'good practice' may be, over and over again.
>
> (p. 168)

It is this kind of relationship-based pedagogy that encourages teachers to explore their own subjectivities by comparing and contrasting their own perspectives with others from both theory and practice. In this way, views are reflected on and reconstructed with relation to specific, context-bound situations. The process is progressive, ever-changing, with current resolutions becoming new starting points for future reflection and change. This is the true challenge of relationship-based approaches to learning and teaching – there is no end – just new and evolving relationships to be created, negotiated and sustained.

References

Ahnert, L., Gunmar, M.R., Lamb, M. and Barthel, M. (2004) Transition to child care: associations with infant–mother attachment, infant negative emotion, and cortisol elevations, *Child Development*, 75: 639–650.

Ahnert, L., Pinquart, M. and Lamb, M.E. (2006) Security of children's relationships with nonparental care providers: a meta-analysis, *Child Development*, 77: 664–679.

Ailwood, J. (2008) Mothers, teachers, maternalism and early childhood education and care: some historical connections, *Contemporary Issues in Early Childhood*, 8: 157–165.

Ainsworth, M. (1979) Infant–mother attachment, *American Psychologist*, 34: 932–937.

Ainsworth, M.D.S., Bell, S.M. and Stayton, D.J. (1974) Infant–mother attachment and social development: socialisation as a product of reciprocal responsiveness to signals, in M.P.M. Richards (ed.) *The Introduction of the Child Into a Social World*. London: Cambridge University Press.

Alasuutari, M. (2010) Striving at partnership: parent–practitioner relationships in Finnish early educators' talk, *European Early Childhood Education Research Journal*, 18: 149–161.

Appleby, K. (2010) Reflective thinking; reflective practice, in M. Reed and N. Canning (eds) *Reflective Practice in the Early Years*. London: Sage.

Auhagen, A.E. and von Salisch, M. (1996) Introduction, in A.E. Auhagen and M.V. Salisch (eds) *The Diversity of Human Relationships*. Cambridge, MA: Cambridge University Press.

Australian Department of Education Employment and Workplace Relations (2009) *Belonging, Belonging and Becoming: the Early Years Learning Framework for Australia*. Canberra: DEEWR.

Avgitidou, S. (2001) Peer culture and friendship relationships as contexts for the development of young children's pro-social behaviour, *International Journal of Early Years Education*, 9: 145–152.

Baker, T. (2009) *The 8 Values of Highly Productive Companies: Creating Wealth From a New Employment Relationship*. Bowen Hills, Australia: Australian Academic Press.

Berthelsen, D. (2010) Introduction, *International Journal of Early Childhood*, 42: 81–86.

Berthelsen, D. and Brownlee, J. (2005) Respecting children's agency for learning and rights to participation in child care programs, *International Journal of Early Childhood*, 37: 49–60.

Berthelsen, D., Brownlee, J. and Boulton-Lewis, G. (2002) Caregivers' epistemological beliefs in toddler programs, *Early Child Development and Care*, 172: 503–516.

Berthelsen, D., Brownlee, J. and Johansson, E. (eds) (2009) *Participatory Learning in the Early Years: Research and Pedagogy*. Oxon, UK: Routledge.

Biesta, G. (2007) Why 'what works' won't work: evidence-based practice and the democratic deficit in educational research, *Educational Theory*, 57: 1–22.

Bove, C. (2001) Inserimento: a strategy for delicately beginning relationships and communications, in L. Gandini and C.P. Edwards (eds) *Bambini: The Italian Approach to Infant/Toddler Care*. New York: Teachers College Press.

Bowlby, J. (1958) The nature of the child's tie to its mother, *International Journal of Psychoanalysis*, 39: 350–373.

Bowlby, J. (1969/2000) *Attachment and Loss, Vol. 1*. New York: Basic Books.

Bradbury, A. (2012) 'I feel absolutely incompetent': professionalism, policy and early childhood teachers, *Contemporary Issues in Early Childhood*, 13: 175–186.

Brecht, G. (1997) *Sorting out Relationships*. Sydney: Prentice Hall.

Bronfenbrenner, U. (1979) *The Ecology of Human Development*. Boston, MA: Harvard University Press.

Brooker, L. (2007) Changing the landscape of early childhood, in J. Moyles (ed.) *Early Years Foundations: Meeting the Challenge*. Maidenhead, UK: Open University Press.

Brooker, L. (2009) Just like having a best friend: how babies and toddlers construct relationships with their key workers in nurseries, in T. Papatheodorou and J. Moyles (eds) *Learning Together in the Early Years: Exploring Relational Pedagogy*. Oxford: Routledge.

Brooker, L. (2010) Constructing the triangle of care: power and professionalism in practitioner/parent relationships, *British Journal of Educational Studies*, 58: 181–196.

Brownell, C.A. (1990) Peer social skills in toddlers: competencies and constraints illustrated by same-age and mixed-age interactions, *Child Development*, 61: 838–848.

Brownell, C.A. and Kopp, C.B. (2007) *Socioemotional Development in the Toddler Years: Transitions and Transformations*. New York: The Guilford Press.

Brownell, C.A., Ramani, G.B. and Zerwas, S. (2006) Becoming a social partner with peers: cooperation and social understanding in one- and two-year-olds, *Child Development*, 77: 803–821.

Brownlee, J. (2001) Knowing and learning in teacher education: a theoretical framework of core and peripheral epistemological beliefs in application, *Asia Pacific Journal of Teacher Education and Development*, 4: 167–190.

Brownlee, J. and Berthelsen, D. (2006) Personal epistemology and relational pedagogy in early childhood teacher education programs, *Early Years: Journal of International Research and Development*, 26: 17–29.

Brownlee, J., Berthelsen, D. and Boulton-Lewis, G. (2004) Working with toddlers in child care: personal epistemologies and practice, *European Early Childhood Education Research Journal*, 12: 55–70.

Bruner, J.S. (1996) *The Culture of Education*. Cambridge, MA: Harvard University Press.

Bruner, J.S. and Sherwood, V. (1976) Peekaboo and the learning of rule structures, in J.S. Bruner, A. Jolly and K. Sylva (eds) *Play: Its Role in Evolution and Development*. London: Penguin Books.

Butterfield, P.M., Martin, C.A. and Prairie, A.P. (2004) *Emotional Connections: How Relationships Guide Early Learning*. Washington, DC: Zero to Three.

Buysse, V. and Wesley, P.W. (2006a) Evidence-based practice: how did it emerge and what does it really mean for the early childhood field, in V. Buysse and P.W. Wesley (eds) *Evidence Based Practice in the Early Childhood Field*. Washington, DC: Zero to Three.

Buysse, V. and Wesley, P.W. (2006b) Preface, in V. Buysse and P.W. Wesley (eds) *Evidence Based Practice in the Early Childhood Field*. Washington, DC: Zero to Three.

Buysse, V., Wesley, P.W., Snyder, P. and Winton, P. (2006) Evidence-based practice: what does it really mean for the early childhood field? *Young Exceptional Children*, 9: 2–11.

Canella, G.S. (1997) *Deconstructing Early Childhood Education: Social Justice and Revolution*. New York: Peter Lang.

Carpendale, J. and Lewis, C. (2006) *How Children Develop Social Understanding*. Oxford: Blackwell Publishing.

Carter, M. and Curtis, D. (1998) *The Visionary Director: A Handbook for Dreaming, Organizing, and Improvising in Your Centre*. St Paul, MN: Redleaf Press.

Centre for Early Childhood Development and Education (2006) *Síolta, the National Quality Framework for Early Childhood Education*. Dublin: CECDE.

Cheeseman, S. (2007) Pedagogical silences in Australian early childhood social policy, *Contemporary Issues in Early Childhood*, 8: 244–254.

Clark, R.M. and Baylis, S. (2012) 'Wasted down there': policy and practice with under-threes, *Early Years: An International Journal of Research and Development*, 32: 229–242.

Corsaro, W.A. (1994) Discussion, debate, and friendship processes: peer discourse in US and Italian nursery schools, *Sociology of Education*, 67: 1–26.

Corsaro, W.A. (2000) Early childhood education, children's peer cultures, and the future of childhood, *European Early Childhood Education Research Journal*, 8: 89–102.

Corsaro, W.A. (2005) *The Sociology of Childhood* (2nd edn). Thousand Oaks, CA: Pine Forge Press.

Corsaro, W.A. (2012) Interpretive reproduction in children's play, *American Journal of Play*, 4: 488–504.

Cortazar, A. and Herreros, F. (2010) Early attachment relationships and the early childhood curriculum, *Contemporary Issues in Early Childhood*, 11: 192–202.

Cryer, D., Wagner-Moore, L., Burchinal, M., Yazejian, N., Hurwitz, S. and Woolery, M. (2005) Effects of transitions to new child care classes on infnat/toddler distress and behavior, *Early Childhood Research Quarterly*, 20: 37–56.

Curtis, D. and Carter, M. (2003) *Design for Living and Learning*. St Paul, MN: Redleaf Press.

Dahlberg, G., Moss, P. and Pence, A. (1999) *Beyond Quality in Early Childhood Education and Care: Postmodern Perspectives*. London: Falmer Press.

Dalli, C. (2000) Starting child care: what young children learn about relating to adults in the first weeks of starting child care, *Early Childhood Research in Practice*, 2.

Dalli, C. (2008) Pedagogy, knowledge and collaboration: towards a ground up perspective on professionalism, *European Early Childhood Education Research Journal*, 16: 171–185.

Datler, W., Ereky-Stevens, K., Hover-Reisner, N. and Malmberg, L.E. (2012) Toddlers' transition to out-of-home care: settling into a new care environment, *Infant Behavior and Development*, 35: 430–451.

Davar, E. (2001) The loss of the transitional object: some thoughts about transitional and 'pre-transitional' phenomena, *Psychodynamic Counselling*, 7: 5–26.

Davidov, M., Zahn-Waxler, C., Roth-Hanania, R. and Knafo, A. (2013) Concern for others in the first year of life: theory, evidence, and avenues for research, *Child Development Perspectives*, 7: 126–131.

Davis, B. and Degotardi, S. (in press) Educators' understandings of, and provisions for, infant peer relationships in early childhood settings, *Journal of Early Childhood Research*.

De Groot Kim, S. (2010) There's Elly, it must be Tuesday: discontinuity in child care programs and its impact on the development of peer relationships in young children, *Early Childhood Education Journal*, 38: 153–164.

De Haan, D. and Singer, E. (2001) Young children's language of togetherness, *International Journal of Early Childhood*, 9: 117–124.

Degotardi, S. (2010) High-quality interactions with infants: relationships with early childhood practitioners' interpretations and qualification levels in play and routine contexts, *International Journal of Early Years Education*, 18: 27–41.

Degotardi, S. (2011a) From greetings to meetings: how infant peers welcome and accommodate a newcomer into their classroom, *The First Years Tga Tua Tuatahi: New Zealand Journal of Infant and Toddler Education*, 13: 29–33.

Degotardi, S. (2011b) Two steps back: exploring identity and presence while observing infants in the nursery, in E. Johansson and E.J.J. White (eds) *Educational Research with Our Youngest*. Dordrecht, Holland: Springer.

Degotardi, S. (2011c) Guest editorial: perspectives and participation in infant–toddler research, *The First Years Tga Tua Tuatahi: New Zealand Journal of Infant and Toddler Education*, 13: 3–4.

Degotardi, S. (2013) 'I think, I can': acknowledging and promoting agency during educator–infant play, in O.F. Lillemyr, S. Dockett and B. Perry (eds) *Varied Perspectives on Play and Learning: Theory and Research on Early Years Education*. Charlotte, NC: Information Age Publishing.

Degotardi, S. (2014) Expressing, interpreting and exchanging perspectives during infant–toddler social interactions: the significance of acting with others in mind, in L. Harrison and J. Sumsion (eds) *Lived Spaces of Infant–Toddler Education and Care: Exploring Diverse Perspectives on Theory, Research, Practice and Policy*. New York: Springer.

Degotardi, S. and Davis, B. (2008) Understanding infants: characteristics of early childhood practitioners' interpretations of infants and their behaviours, *Early Years: An International Journal of Research and Development*, 28: 221–234.

Degotardi, S. and Pearson, E. (2009) Relationship theory in the nursery: attachment and beyond, *Contemporary Issues in Early Childhood*, 10: 144–145.

Degotardi, S. and Pearson, E. (2010) Knowing me, knowing you: the relationship dynamics of infant play, in M. Ebbeck and M. Waniganayake (eds) *Play in Early Childhood Education: Learning in Diverse Contexts*. Melbourne: Oxford University Press.

Degotardi, S. and Sweller, N. (2012) Mind-mindedness in infant child-care: associations with early childhood practitioner sensitivity and stimulation, *Early Childhood Research Quarterly*, 27: 253–265.

Degotardi, S., Semann, A. and Shepherd, W. (2012) Using practitioner inquiry to promote reflexivity and change in early childhood programs, in P. Whiteman and K. De Gioia (eds) *Children and Childhoods*. Newcastle, UK: Cambridge Scholars Publishing.

Degotardi, S., Sweller, N. and Pearson, E. (2013) Why relationships matter: parent and early childhood teacher perspectives about the provisions afforded by young children's relationships, *International Journal of Early Years Education*, 21: 4–12.

Department for Education and Skills (2002) *Birth to Three Matters: A Framework to Support Children in Their Earliest Years*. London: DfES/Surestart.

Department for Education and Skills (2007) *Early Years Foundation Stage: Setting the Standards for Learning, Development and Care for Children From Birth to Five*. London: DfEs/Sure Start.

Department of Education (2012) *Statutory Framework for Early Years Foundation Stage: Setting the Standards for Learning, Development and Care for Children From Birth to Five*. London: Department of Education.

Deynoot-Schaub, M. and Risken-Walraven, J. (2006) Peer interaction in child care centres at 15 and 23 months: stability and links with children's socio-economic adjustment, *Infant Behavior and Development*, 29: 276–288.

Duck, S. (1998) *Human Relationships*. London: Sage.

Duck, S. (1999) *Relating to Others*. Buckingham, UK: Open University Press.

Dunn, J. (1994) Changing minds and relationships, in C. Lewis and P. Mitchell (eds) *Children's Understanding of Mind: Origins and Development*. Hove, UK: Erlbaum.

Dunn, J. (2004) *Children's Friendships: The Beginning of Intimacy*. Oxford: Wiley Blackwell.

Durden, T. and Dangel, J.R. (2008) Teacher-involved conversations with young children during small group activity, *Early Years: Journal of International Research and Development*, 28: 251–266.

Ebbeck, M. and Yim, B. (2008) Rethinking attachment: fostering positive relationships between infants, toddlers and their primary caregivers, *Early Child Development and Care*, 197: 899–909.

Eckerman, C.O. and Whatley, J.L. (1977) Toys and social interaction between infant peers, *Child Development*, 48: 1645–1656.

Elfer, P. (2007) Nurseries and emotional well-being: evaluating an emotionally containing model of professional development, *Early Years: An International Journal of Research and Development*, 27: 267–279.

Elfer, P. (2012) Emotion in nursery work: work discussion as a model of critical professional reflection, *Early Years: An International Journal of Research and Development*, 32, 129–141.

Elicker, J., Noppe, L.C., Noppe, L.D. and Fortner-Wood, C. (1997) The parent–caregiver relationship scale: rounding out the relationship system in infant child care, *Early Education and Development*, 8: 83–100.

Eliot, T.S. (1942) *Four Quartets (#4 Little Gidding)*. London: Faber & Faber.

Emde, R.N. (2009) Facilitating reflective supervision in an early child development centre, *Infant Mental Health Journal*, 30: 664–672.

Engdahl, I. (2011) Toddler interaction during play in the Swedish preschool, *Early Child Development and Care*, 181: 1421–1439.

Engdahl, I. (2012) Doing friendship during the second year of life in a Swedish preschool, *European Early Childhood Education Research Journal*, 20: 83–98.

Fein, G.G., Gariboldi, A. and Raffaella, B. (1993) The adjustment of infants and toddlers to group care: the first 6 months, *Early Childhood Research Quarterly*, 8: 1–14.

Fenech, M., Sumsion, J. and Shepherd, W. (2010) Promoting early childhood teacher professionalism in the Australian context: the place of resistance, *Contemporary Issues in Early Childhood*, 11: 89–104.

Finkelstein, N.W., Dent, C., Gallacher, K. and Ramey, C.T. (1978) Social behaviour of infants and toddlers in a day-care environment, *Developmental Psychology*, 14: 257–262.

Forgas, J.P. and Fitness, J. (eds) (2008) *Social Relationships: Cognitive, Affective, and Motivational Processes*. New York: Psychology Press.

Fox, M. (2011) Practice-based evidence – overcoming insecure attachments, *Educational Psychology in Practice: Theory, Research and Practice in Educational Psychology*, 27: 325–335.

Gillespie, A. (2006) Games and the development of perspective taking, *Human Development*, 49: 87–92.

Gonzalez-Mena, J. (2010) *Diversity in Early Care and Education* (5th edn). New York: NAEYC.

Gonzalez-Mena, J. and Widmeyer Eyer, D. (2007) *Infants, Toddlers, and Caregivers: A Curriculum of Respectful, Responsive Care and Education*. Boston, MA: McGraw-Hill.

Goouch, K. and Powell, S. (2013) *The Baby Room: Principles, Policies and Practice*. Maidenhead: Open University Press.

Greenman, J., Stonehouse, A. and Schweikert, G. (2008) *Prime Times: A Handbook for Excellence in Infant and Toddler Programs*. St Paul, MN: Redleaf Press.

Gudykunst, W.B., Ting-Toomey, S. and Nishida, T. (eds) (1996) *Communication in Personal Relationships Across Cultures*. Thousand Oaks, CA: Sage.

Hännikäinen, M. (1999) Togetherness – a manifestation of day care life, *Early Child Development and Care*, 151: 19–28.

Hännikäinen, M. (2001) Playful actions as a sign of togetherness in day care centres, *International Journal of Early Years Education*, 9.

Hännikäinen, M. and Rutanen, N. (2013) Important themes in research on and education of young children in day care centres: Finnish viewpoints, *Nordisk Barnehageforskning*, 6: 1–10.

Harrison, L. and Sumsion, J. (eds) (2014) *Lived Spaces of Infant–Toddler Education and Care: Exploring Diverse Perspectives on Theory, Research, Practice and Policy*. New York: Springer.

Harrist, A.W., Thompson, S.D. and Norris, D.J. (2007) Defining quality child care: multiple stakeholder perspectives, *Early Education and Development*, 18: 305–336.

Hay, D.F., Caplan, M. and Nash, A. (2009) The beginnings of peer relations, in K. Rubin, W.M. Bukowski and B. Laurson (eds) *Handbook of Peer Interactions, Relationships, and Groups*. New York: The Guilford Press.

Hay, D.F., Nash, A. and Pederson, J. (1983) Interaction between six-month-olds peers, *Child Development*, 54: 557–562.

Hay, D.F., Payne, A. and Chadwick, A. (2004) Peer relations in early childhood, *Journal of Child Psychology and Psychiatry*, 45: 84–108.

Hedges, H. (2012) Teachers' funds of knowledge: a challenge to evidence based practice, *Teachers and Teaching: Theory and Practice*, 18: 7–24.

Hinde, R.A. (1979) *Towards Understanding Relationships*. London: Academic Press.

Hinde, R.A. (1997) *Relationships: A Dialectical Perspective*. Hove, UK: Psychology Press.

Hohmann, U. (2007) Rights, expertise and negotiations in care and education, *Early Years: An International Journal of Research and Development*, 27: 33–46.

Honneth, A. (1995) *The Struggle for Recognition: The Moral Grammar of Social Conflicts*. Cambridge: Polity Press.

Howes, C. (1996) The earliest friendships, in W.M. Bukowski, A.F. Newcomb and W.H. Hartup (eds) *The Company They Keep: Friendship in Childhood and Adolescence*. New York: Cambridge University Press.

Howes, C. (2008) Friends and peers, in M.M. Haith and J.B. Benson (eds) *Encyclopedia of Infant and Early Childhood Development*. Houston, TX: Academic Press.

Howes, C. (2009) Friendship in early childhood, in K.H. Rubin, W.M. Bukowski and B. Laurson (eds) *Handbook of Peer Interactions, Relationships and Groups*. New York: New Guilford Press.

Howes, C., Hamilton, C.C. and Hamilton, C.E. (1994) Maternal, teacher, and child care history correlates of children's relationships with peers, *Child Development*, 65: 264–273.

Howes, C., Hamilton, C.C. and Philipsen, L.C. (1998) Stability and continuity of child–caregiver and child–peer relationships, *Child Development*, 69: 418–426.

Howes, C., Matheson, C. and Hamilton, C.E. (1992) Sequences in the development of competent play with peers: social and social-pretend play, *Developmental Psychology*, 28: 961–974.

Hujala, E., Turja, L., Gaspar, M.F., Veisson, M. and Waniganayake, M. (2009) Perspectives of early childhood teachers on parent–teacher partnerships in five European countries, *European Early Childhood Education Research Journal*, 17: 57–76.

Insley, K. and Lucas, S. (2009) Making the most of the relationship between two adults to impact on early childhood pedagogy: raising standards and narrowing attainment, in T. Papatheodorou and J. Moyles (eds) *Learning Together in the Early Years: Exploring Relational Pedagogy*. London: Routledge.

Ireland, L. (2006) *When Babies Have Teachers: A Study of How Three Community-based Children's Services Employ Teachers in Infant–Toddler Programs*. Adelaide, SA: Australian Association for Research in Education.

Jacobson, J.L. (1981) The role of inanimate objects in early peer interaction, *Child Development*, 52: 618–626.

Johansson, E. (2011) Introduction: giving words to children's voices in research, in E. Johansson and E.J. White (eds) *Educational Research With Our Youngest: Voices of Infants and Toddlers*. Dordrecht, Holland: Springer.

Johansson, E. and White, E.J. (eds) (2011) *Educational Research With Our Youngest: Voices of Infants and Toddlers.* Dordrecht, Holland: Springer.

Jovanovic, J. (2011) Saying goodbye: an investigation into parent–infant separation behaviours on arrival in childcare, *Child Care in Practice,* 17: 247–269.

Jung, J. (2011) Caregivers' playfulness and infants' emotional stress during transitional time, *Early Child Development and Care,* 181: 1397–1407.

Kâğitçibaşi, C. (2007) *Family, Self and Human Development Across Cultures: Theory and Applications.* Hillsdale, NJ: Lawrence Erlbaum.

Kâğıtçıbaşı, C., Sunar, D. and Bekman, S. (2001) Long-term effects of early intervention: Turkish low-income mothers and children. *Journal of Applied Developmental Psychology,* 22: 333–361.

Kâğitçibaşi, C., Sunar, D., Bekman, S., Baydar, N. and Cemalcilar, Z. (2009) Continuing effects of early enrichment in adult life: the Turkish Early Enrichment Project 22 years later, *Journal of Applied Developmental Psychology,* 30(6): 764–779.

Keyes, C.R. (2002) A way of thinking about parent/teacher partnerships for teachers, *International Journal of Early Years Education,* 10: 177–191.

Kim, M.H. and Moon, H. (2011) Infants' social-emotional adjustment within a childcare context of Korea, *Asia Pacific Journal of Education,* 31: 487–502.

Klein, P.S., Kraft, R.R. and Shohet, C. (2010) Behaviour patterns in daily mother–child separations: possible opportunities for stress reduction, *Early Child Development and Care,* 180: 387–396.

Koren-Karie, N., Oppenheim, D., Dolev, S., Sher, E. and Etzion-Carasso, A. (2002) Mothers' insightfulness regarding their infants' internal experience: relations with maternal sensitivity and infant attachment, *Developmental Psychology,* 38: 534–542.

Lally, R.J. (2006) Metatheories of childrearing, in R.F. Lally, P.L. Mangione and D. Greenwald (eds) *Concepts for Care: 20 Essays on Infant/Toddler Development and Learning.* San Francisco, CA: WestEd.

Lamb, M.E. (2005) Attachments, social networks, and developmental contexts, *Human Development,* 48: 108–112.

Lamb, M.E., Bornstein, M.H. and Teti, D.M. (2002) *Development in Infancy.* New York: Psychology Press.

Learning and Teaching Scotland (2010) *Pre-birth to Three: Positive Outcomes for Scotland's Children and Families.* Glasgow: Scottish Government.

Lee, S.Y. (2006) A journey to a close, secure, and synchronous relationship. Infant–caregiver relationship development in a childcare context, *Journal of Early Childhood Research,* 4: 133–151.

Lee, Y.C. and Jessee, P.O. (1997) Taiwanese infants' and toddlers' interactions with a baby in a group setting, *Early Child Development and Care,* 134: 75–87.

Lewis, M. (2005) The child and its family: the social network model, *Human Development,* 48: 8–27.

Licht, B., Simoni, H. and Perrig-Chiello, P. (2008) Conflict between peers in infancy and toddler age: what do they fight about? *Early Years*, 1: 1–15.

Loizou, E. (2007) Humour: a different type of play, *European Early Childhood Education Research Journal*, 13: 97–109.

Løkken, G. (2000) Tracing the social style of toddler peers, *Scandinavian Journal of Educational Research*, 44: 163–176.

Løkken, G. (2009) The construction of 'toddler' in early childhood pedagogy, *Contemporary Issues in Early Childhood*, 10: 35–42.

Malaguzzi, L. (1998) History, ideas, and basic philosophy: an interview with Lella Gandini, in C. Edwards, L. Gandini and G. Forman (eds) *The Hundred Languages of Children: The Reggio Emilia Approach – Advanced Reflections* (2nd edn). Greenwich, CT: Ablex.

Mamali, C. (1996) Interpersonal communication in totalitarian societies, in W.B. Gudykunst, S. Ting-Toomey and T. Nishida (eds) *Communication in Personal Relationships Across Cultures*. Thousand Oaks, CA: Sage.

Manning-Morton, J. (2006) The personal is professional: professionalism and the birth to threes practitioner, *Contemporary Issues in Early Childhood*, 7: 42–52.

May, H. (2007) 'Minding', 'working', 'teaching': childcare in Aotearoa/New Zealand, 1940s–2000s, *Contemporary Issues in Early Childhood*, 8: 133–143.

McElwain, N.L., Booth-Laforce, C. and Wu, X. (2011) Infant–mother attachment and children's friendship quality: maternal mental-state talk as an intervening mechanism, *Developmental Psychology*, 47: 1295–1311.

McElwain, N.L., Cox, M.J., Burchinal, M. and Macfie, J. (2003) Differentiating among insecure mother–infant attachment classifications: a focus on child–friend interactions and exploration during solitary play at 36 months, *Attachment and Human Development*, 5: 136–164.

McGaha, C.G., Cummings, R., Lippard, B. and Dallas, K. (2012) Relationship building: infants, toddlers, and 2-year-olds, *Early Childhood Research and Practice*, 13: 1–14.

McHale, J.P. (2007) When infants grow up in multiperson relationship systems, *Infant Mental Health Journal*, 28: 370–392.

Mead, G.H. (1934) *Mind, Self and Society*. London: University of Chicago.

Meeuwig, M. (2008) Child care centres as living and learning communities, *Early Childhood Matters*, 111: 18–23.

Meier, A. and Rovers, M. (2010) *The Helping Relationship: Healing and Change in Community Context*. Ottawa: University of Ottawa Press.

Meins, E., Fernyhough, C., Fradley, E. and Tuckey, M. (2001) Rethinking maternal sensitivity: mothers' comments on infants' mental processes predict security of attachment at 12 months, *Journal of Child Psychology and Psychiatry and Allied Disciplines*, 42: 637–648.

Meins, E., Fernyhough, C., Russell, J. and Clark-Carter, D. (1998) Security of attachment as a predictor of symbolic and mentalising abilities: a longitudinal study, *Social Development*, 7: 1–24.

Meuller, E. and Brenner, J. (1977) The origins of social skills and interaction among playgroup toddlers, *Child Development*, 48: 854–861.

Milne, A.A. (1926) *Winnie the Pooh*. New York: Dutton Children's Books, Penguin Group.

Ministry of Education (1996) *Te Whāriki: He whariki matauranga mo nga mokopuna o Aotearoa. Early childhood curriculum*. Wellington, NZ: Learning Media.

Ministry of Education National Heritage Culture and Arts (2008) *Na Noda Mataniciva*. Republic of Fiji Islands: Ministry of Education, National Heritage, Culture and Arts.

Moll, L.C., Amanti, C., Neff, D. and Gonzalez, N. (1992) Funds of knowledge for teaching: using a qualitative approach to connect homes, *Theory into Practice*, 31: 132–141.

Money, R. (2005) The RIE early years 'curriculum', in S. Petri and S. Owen (eds) *Authentic Relationships in Group Care for Infants and Toddlers: Resources for Infant Educarer (RIE) Principles into Practice*. London: Jessica Kingley Publishers.

Moore, T. (2007) The nature and role of relationships in early childhood intervention services. Second Conference of the International Society on Early Intervention, Zagreb, Croatia.

Moss, P. (2006) Structures, understandings and discourses: possibilities for re-envisioning the early childhood worker, *Contemporary Issues in Early Childhood*, 7: 30–41.

Moss, P. (2007) Bringing politics into the nursery: early childhood education as a democratic practice, *European Early Childhood Education Research Journal*, 15: 5–20.

Moss, P. (2010) We cannot continue as we are: the educator in an education for survival, *Contemporary Issues in Early Childhood*, 11: 8–19.

Musatti, T. and Panni, S. (1981) Social behavior and interaction among day-care center toddlers, *Early Child Development and Care*, 7: 5–27.

National Institute of Child Health and Human Development Early Child Care Research Network (2001) Child care and children's peer interaction at 24 and 36 months: the NICHD Study of early child care, *Child Development*, 72: 1478–1500.

National Scientific Council on the Developing Child (2004) Young children develop in an environment of relationships. Working paper 1. Centre on the Developing Child, Harvard University, online at: http://developingchild.harvard.edu/index.php/resources/reports_and_working_papers/working_papers/wp1/ (accessed August 2013).

National Scientific Council on the Developing Child (2007) The science of early childhood development: closing the gap between what we know and what we do, Harvard University, online at: http://developingchild.harvard.edu/index.php/download_file/-/view/67/%E2%80%8E (accessed August 2013).

Nelson, K. (2007) *Young Minds in Social Worlds: Experience, Meaning, and Memory*. Cambridge, MA: Harvard University Press.

Newport, S.F. (2000) Early childhood care, work, and family in Japan: trends in a society of smaller families, *Childhood Education*, 77: 68.

Noller, P., Feeney, J.A. and Peterson, C. (2001) *Personal Relationships Across the Lifespan*. Hove, UK: Psychology Press.

Nutbrown, C. and Page, J. (2008) *Working with Children from Birth to Three*. Los Angeles: Sage.

Oberhuemer, P. (2012) Editorial, *Early Years: An International Journal of Research and Development*, 32: 109–112.

Organisation for Economic Co-operation and Development (OECD) (2006) *Starting Strong II: Early Childhood Education and Care*. Paris: OECD.

Osgood, J. (2010) Reconstructing professionalism in ECEC: the case for the 'critically reflective emotional professional', *Early Years: An International Research Journal*, 30: 119–133.

Owen, M.T., Ware, A.M. and Barfoot, B. (2000) Caregiver–mother partnership behavior and the quality of caregiver–child and mother–child interactions, *Early Childhood Research Quarterly*, 15: 413–428.

Page, J. (2011) Do mothers want professional carers to love their babies? *Journal of Early Childhood Research*, 9: 310–323.

Page, J., Clare, A. and Nutbrown, C. (2013) *Working with Babies and Children from Birth to Three*. London: Sage.

Paley, V.G. (1986) *Mollie is Three: Growing Up in School*. Chicago: University of Chicago Press.

Papatheodorou, T. (2009) Exploring relational pedagogy, in T. Papatheodorou and J. Moyles (eds) *Learning Together in the Early Years: Exploring Relational Pedagogy*. Oxon, UK: Routledge.

Papatheodorou, T. and Moyles, J. (2009) *Learning Together in the Early Years: Exploring Relational Pedagogy*. Oxon, UK: Routledge.

Pearson, E. (2011) Meetings, greetings and the role of broader social contexts: a 'response', *The First Years Tga Tua Tuatahi: New Zealand Journal of Infant and Toddler Education*, 13: 34–35.

Pirard, F. and Barbier, J.M. (2012) Accompaniment and quality in the emergence of a culture of professionalization, *Early Years: An International Journal of Research and Development*, 32, 171–182.

Raikes, H.H, Edwards, C.P. and Gandini, L. (2009) *Extending the Dance in Infant and Toddler Caregiving: Enhancing Attachment and Relationships*. Baltimore, MD: Brookes Publishing.

Rayna, S. (2001) The very beginnings of togetherness in shared play among young children, *International Journal of Early Years Education*, 9: 109–115.

Rayna, S. and Laevers, F. (2011) Understanding children from 0–3 years of age and its implications for education. what's new on the babies' side? Origins and evolutions, *European Early Childhood Education Research Journal*, 19: 161–172.

Recchia, S.L. (2012) Caregiver–child relationships as a context for continuity in child care, *Early Years: An International Journal of Research and Development*, 32: 143–157.

Recchia, S.L. and Dvorakova, K. (2012) How three young toddlers transition from an infant to a toddler child care classroom: exploring the influence of peer relationships, teacher expectations, and changing social contexts, *Early Education and Development*, 23: 181–201.

Recchia, S.L. and Shin, M.S. (2012) In and out of synch: infant childcare teachers' adaptations to infants' developmental changes, *Early Child Development and Care*, 182: 1545–1562.

Reddy, V. (2008) *How Infants Know Minds*. Cambridge, MA: Harvard University Press.

Rinaldi, C. (2001) Reggio Emilia: the image of the child and the child's environment as a fundamental principle, in L. Gandini and C. Pope Edwards (eds) *Bambini: The Italian Approach to Infant/Toddler Care*. New York: Teachers College Press.

Rochat, P. (2001) *The Infant's World*. Cambridge, MA: Harvard University Press.

Rochat, P. (2009) *Others in Mind: Social Origins of Self-consciousness*. Cambridge, UK: Cambridge University Press.

Rockel, J. (2005) Primary care in early childhood education – to be or not to be? *ACE Papers*: 73–87.

Rockel, J. (2009) A pedagogy of care: moving beyond the margins of managing work and minding babies, *Australasian Journal of Early Childhood*, 34: 1–8.

Rockel, J. and Craw, J. (2011) Discourse of happiness in infant–toddler pedagogy, *New Zealand Research in Early Childhood Education Journal*, 14: 121–131.

Rogoff, B. (1998) Cognition as a collaborative process, in W. Damon (ed.) *Handbook of Child Psychology* (5th edn). New York: Wiley.

Rogoff, B. (2003) *The Cultural Nature of Human Development*. New York: Oxford University Press.

Rolfe, S.A. (2004) *Rethinking Attachment for Early Childhood Practice: Promoting Security, Autonomy and Resilience in Young Children*. Crows Nest, NSW: Allen & Unwin.

Rose-Krasnor, L. and Denham, S. (2009) Social-emotional competence in early childhood, in J.H. Rubin, W.M. Bukawski and B. Laursen (eds) *Handbook of Peer Interactions, Relationships, and Groups*. New York, NY: The Guilford Press.

Rutanen, N. (2012) Socio-spacial practices in a Finnish daycare group for one- to three-year-olds, *Early Years*, 32: 201–214.

Rutanen, N. (2014) Lived spaces in a toddler group: application of Lefebvre's spatial triad, in L. Harrison and J. Sumsion (eds) *Lived Spaces of Infant–Toddler Education and Care: Exploring Diverse Perspectives on Theory, Research, Practice and Policy*. New York: Springer.

Sachs, J. (2003) *The Activist Teaching Profession*. Buckingham, UK: Open University Press.

Salamon, A. (2011) How the Early Years Learning Framework can help shift pervasive beliefs of the social and emotional capablities of infants and toddlers, *Contemporary Issues in Early Childhood*, 12: 4–10.

Selby, J. and Bradley, B. (2003) Infants in groups: a paradigm for the study of early social experience, *Human Development*, 46: 197–221.

Shier, H. (2001) Pathways to participation: opening, opportunities and obligations, *Children and Society*, 15: 107–117.

Shin, M. (2012) The role of joint attention in social communication and play among infants, *Journal of Early Childhood Research*, 10: 309–317.

Shin, M., Recchia, S.L., Lee, S.Y., Lee, Y.J. and Mullarkey, S.L. (2004) Understanding early childhood leadership: emerging competencies in the context of relationships, *Journal of Early Childhood Research*, 2: 301–316.

Shonkoff, J.P. (2006) Foreword, in V. Buysse and P.W. Wesley (eds) *Evidence-based Practice in the Early Childhood Field*. Washington, DC: Zero to Three.

Shonkoff, J.P. (2010) Building a new biodevelopmental framework to guide the future of early childhood policy, *Child Development*, 81: 357–367.

Shonkoff, J.P. and Phillips, D.A. (2000) *From Neurones to Neighbourhoods: The Science of Early Childhood Development*. Washington, DC: National Academy Press.

Shore, L.M., Coyle-Shapiro, J.A. and Tetrick, L.E. (2012) *The Employee–organization Relationship: Applications for the 21st Century*. New York: Routledge.

Shpancer, N. (2002) The home–daycare link: mapping children's new world order, *Early Childhood Research Quarterly*, 17: 374–392.

Shweder, R.A., Goodnow, J., Hatano, G., Levine, R.A., Markus, H. and Miller, P. (1998) The cultural psychology of development: one mind, many mentalities, in W. Damon (ed.) *Handbook of Child Psychology*. New York: Wiley.

Sims, M. and Hutchins, T. (2011) *Program Planning for Infants and Toddlers: In Search of Relationships*. Castle Hill, NSW: Pademelon Press.

Singer, E. and De Haan, D. (2007) Social life of young children: co-construction of shared meanings and togetherness, humour, and conflicts in child care centres, in B. Spodek and O.N. Saracho (eds) *Contemporary Perspectives on Research in Early Childhood Social Learning*. Charlotte, NC: Information Age Publishers.

Siraj-Blatchford, I., Taggart, B., Sylva, K., Sammons, P. and Melhuish, E. (2008) Towards the transformation of practice in early childhood education: the Effective Provision of Pre-School Education (EPPE) project, *Cambridge Journal of Education*, 38: 23–36.

Smith, A.B. (1999) Quality childcare and joint attention, *International Journal of Early Years Education*, 7: 85–98.

Smith, A.B. (2011) Respecting children's rights and agency: theoretical insights into ethical research procedures, in D. Harcourt, B. Perry, and T. Waller, (eds) *Researching Young Children's Perspectives: Debating the Ethics and Dilemmas of Educational Research with Children*. London: Routledge.

Sumsion, J. (2005) Staff shortages in children's services: challenging taken-for-granted discourses, *Australian Journal of Early Childhood*, 30: 40–48.

Sumsion, J. and Wong, S. (2011) Interrogating 'Belonging' in Belonging, Being and Becoming: The Early Years Learning Framework for Australia, *Contemporary Issues in Early Childhood*, 12: 28–45.

Sumsion, J., Barnes, S., Cheeseman, S., Harrison, L., Kennedy, A. and Stonehouse, A. (2009) Insider perspectives on developing Belonging, Being and Becoming: The Early Years Learning Framework for Australia, *Australasian Journal of Early Childhood*, 34: 4–13.

Super, C.M. and Harkness, S. (1986) The developmental niche: a conceptualization at the interface of child and culture, *International Journal of Behavioral Development*, 9: 545–569.

Taggart, G. (2011) Don't we care? The ethics and emotional labour of early year professionalism, *Early Years: An International Journal of Research and Development*, 31: 85–95.

Takahashi, K. (2005) Towards a life span theory of close relationships: the affective relationships model, *Human Development*, 48: 48–66.

Tamis-LeMonda, C.S. (1996) Introduction: maternal sensitivity: individual, contextual and cultural factors in recent conceptualizations, *Early Development and Parenting*, 5: 167–171.

Taumoepeau, M. and Ruffman, T. (2008) Stepping stones to others' minds: maternal talk relates to child mental state language and emotion understanding at 15, 24, and 33 months, *Child Development*, 79: 284–302.

Thompson, R.A. (2005) Multiple relationships multiply considered, *Human Development*, 48: 102–107.

Thyssen, S. (2010) Child culture, play and child development, *Early Child Development and Care*, 173: 589–612.

United Nations (1989) *Convention on the Rights of the Child*. Geneva: United Nations.

Urban, M. (2008) Dealing with uncertainty: challenges and possibilities for the early childhood profession, *European Early Childhood Education Research Journal*, 16: 135–152.

Urban, M. (2010) Zones of professional development: arguments for reclaiming practice-based evidence in early childhood practice and research, in A. Tina and J. Hayden (eds) *Early Childhood Programs as the Doorway to Social Cohesion*. Newcastle upon Tyne, UK: Cambridge Scholars Publishing.

Urban, M. and Dalli, C. (2012) A profession speaking and thinking for itself, in L. Miller, C. Dalli and M. Urban (eds) *Early Childhood Grows Up: International Perspectives on Early Childhood Education and Development*. Dordrecht, Holland: Springer.

Van Oers, B. and Hännikäinen, M. (2001) Some thoughts about togetherness: an introduction, *International Journal of Early Years Education*, 9: 101–108.

Vandell, D.L., Wilson, K.S. and Buchanan, N.R. (1980) Peer interaction in the first year of life: an examination of its structure, content, and sensitivity to toys, *Child Development*, 51: 481–488.

Vandenbroeck, M. (2009) Let us disagree, *European Early Childhood Education Research Journal*, 17: 165–170.

Vangelisti, A.L. and Perlman, D. (eds) (2006) *The Cambridge Handbook of Personal Relationships*. Cambridge, UK: Cambridge University Press.

Virmani, E.A. and Ontai, L.L. (2010) Supervision and training in child care: does reflective supervision foster caregiver insightfulness? *Infant Mental Health Journal*, 31: 16–32.

Vygotsky, L.S. (1978) *Mind in Society: The Development of Higher Mental Function*. Cambridge, MA: Harvard University Press.

Weatherston, D., Weigand, R.F. and Weigand, B. (2010) Reflective supervision: supporting reflection as a cornerstone for competency, *Zero to Three*, 31: 22–30.

Weiss, R. (1974) The provisions of social relationships, in Z. Rubin (ed.) *Doing Unto Others: Joining, Molding, Conforming, Helping, Loving*. Englewood Cliffs, NJ: Prentice-Hall.

Welsh, I.D. (2003) *The Therapeutic Relationship: Listening and Responing in a Multicultural World*. Westport, CT: Praeger.

Whaley, K.L. and Rubenstein, T.S. (1994) How toddlers 'do' friendship: a descriptive analysis of naturally occurring friendships in a group child care setting, *Journal of Social and Personal Relationships*, 11: 383–400.

Whipple, N., Bernier, A. and Mageau, G. (2011) Broadening the study of infant security of attachment: maternal autonomy-support in the context of infant exploration, *Social Development*, 20: 17–32.

White, E.J. (2011) Summary: lessons learnt and future provications, in E. Johansson and E.J. White (eds) *Educational Research With Our Youngest: Voices of Infants and Toddlers*. Dordrecht, Holland: Springer.

Whiting, B.B. and Whiting, J.W.M. (1975) *Children of Six Cultures: A Psycho-cultural Analysis*. Cambridge, MA: Harvard University Press.

Williams, S.T., Mastergeorge, A.M. and Ontai, L.L. (2010) Caregiver involvement in infant peer interactions: scaffolding in a social context, *Early Childhood Research Quarterly*, 25: 251–266.

Winton, P.J. (2006) The evidence-based practice movement and its effect on knowledge utilisation, in V. Buysse and P.W. Wesley (eds) *Evidence-based Practice in the Early Childhood Field*. Washington, DC: Zero to Three.

Wittmer, D. (2008) *Focusing on Peers: The Importance of Relationships in the Early Years*. Washington, DC: Zero to Three.

Wittmer, D.S. and Petersen, S.H. (2009) *Endless Opportunities for Infant and Toddler Curriculum: A Relationship-based Approach*. New Jersey: Pearson.

Wong, S. (2007) Looking back and moving forward: historicising the social construction of early childhood education and care as national work, *Contemporary Issues in Early Childhood*, 8: 144–156.

Wood, D., Bruner, J.S. and Ross, G. (1976) The role of tutoring in problem solving, *Journal of Child Psychiatry and Psychology*, 17: 89–100.

Woodhead, M. and Brooker, L. (2008) A sense of belonging, *Early Childhood Matters*, 111: 3–6.

Woodrow, C. (2008) Discourses of professional identity in early childhood: movements in Australia, *European Early Childhood Education Research Journal*, 16: 269–280.

Index

DOING ETHICAL RESEARCH WITH CHILDREN

Deborah Harcourt and Jonathon Sargeant

9780335246427 (Paperback)

August 2012

eBook also available

Doing Ethical Research with Children introduces students to the key considerations involved when researching with children and young people, from both a methodological and ethical perspective. It will assist students as they develop, conduct and disseminate research that relates to children and childhood.

Key features:

- Combines appropriate and supportive information to offer a guide through the issues and essential elements of conducting ethical research with children
- Includes pedagogical features throughout to develop understanding
- Different stages of research are covered, from planning the research to carrying out the study

www.openup.co.uk

 OPEN UNIVERSITY PRESS
McGraw - Hill Education

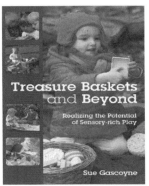

TREASURE BASKETS AND BEYOND
Realizing the Potential of Sensory-rich Play

Sue Gascoyne

9780335246441 (Paperback)
2012

eBook also available

"This accomplished book represents an impressive and important
extension of previous writing in the field and is sure to expand
practitioners' understanding of the fascinating medium that is the
treasure basket."
Janet Moyles, Professor Emeritus, Anglia Ruskin University, UK

Watching a child play with a Treasure Basket can give a powerful insight
into the wonder of children's minds; their developmental levels, interests,
likes and dislikes; repeated patterns of behaviour; and even glimpses of a
child's personality. This book draws extensively upon observations of
children's play as well as contemporary and original research in
neuroscience and sensory play, to offer fresh insights into the use and
benefits of Treasure Baskets and sensory-rich play.

Key features:

- Explaining the importance of sensory play in terms of its powerful
  effect upon brain development and memory
- The problem solving potential of sensory rich play

www.openup.co.uk

OPEN UNIVERSITY PRESS
McGraw - Hill Education

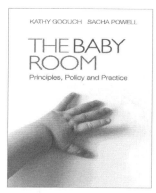

THE BABY ROOM
Principles, Policy and Practice

Kathy Goouch & Sacha Powell

9780335246366 (Paperback)
2013

eBook also available

This book considers babies' development with a view to disseminating good practice in out-of-home daycare for babies and young children. It is informed by a research and development project - the Baby Room Project - which examined the practices, attitudes and qualifications of those working with the youngest children in formal daycare settings.
Drawing on unique snapshots of practice and original research evidence the book considers development issues related to the care of babies and creates a 'Baby Room Charter'.

Key features:

- The book is informed by a research and development project carried out called The Baby Room Project
- Although a staggering 43% of babies are cared for outside of the home in the UK, there has been little or no research undertaken in relation to the care of babies in nurseries until now
- A variety of detailed information from the range of international research on babies' development and care

www.openup.co.uk

 OPEN UNIVERSITY PRESS
McGraw - Hill Education

A-Z OF PLAY IN EARLY CHILDHOOD

Janet Moyles

9780335246380 (Paperback)
2012

eBook also available

This indispensable guide uses a unique glossary format to explore some of the key themes in play in early childhood, many of which regularly arise for students, tutors, parents and practitioners. As well as covering key concepts, theories and influential figures in the field, the book considers important aspects of each construct and highlights the complexity of play in early childhood.

Key features:

- Split into a comprehensive glossary running through elements of play from A – Z, it is a useful, fun and unique companion to understanding children's play
- Original thoughts from well known early years people including Tricia David, Carol Aubrey, Angela Anning and Lilian Katz

www.**openup**.co.uk

 OPEN UNIVERSITY PRESS
McGraw - Hill Education